To friend Fran Fontana

Best all ways, always.

Miriam

THE

AROUND THE RIM

FLIGHT

*There is a certain blend of courage,
integrity, character and principle which has
no satisfactory dictionary name but has been
called different things at different times in
different cultures.*

Our American name for it is "guts".

Louis Adamic

THE

AROUND THE RIM

FLIGHT

By

Miriam Orr Seymour

First Edition

Running Iron
Publications
PO Box 12755
Prescott, AZ 86304

i

Copyright © 2002, Miriam Orr Seymour

ISBN (Hardcover) 0-917882-52-0
ISBN (Paperback) 0-917882-51-2

Printed in the United States of America
First printing: 2002.

Library of Congress Cataloging-in-Publication Data

Seymour, Miriam Orr, 1922 –
    The around the rim flight / by Miriam Orr Seymour.—1st ed.
        p. cm.
    Includes bibliographical references and index.
    ISBN 0-917882-52-0 (hc.) – ISBN 0-917882-51-2 (pbk.)
        1. Transcontinental flights—United States. 2. United
            States. Army. Air Service. I. Title.

TL721.U58 S49 2002
619.13'0973—dc21

SPECIAL THANKS

To: Writer and Aviation Historian Merle C. Olmsted

  For inspiration and invaluable assistance

To: The "Jerry" Dobias family

  For sharing memories and memorabilia

To: Best selling author Robert J. Serling

  For making time to write the Foreword

To: Artist Herbert C. Greif

  For the cover design and fine drawings

To: The literate Lansers, Marilyn and Joe

  For constructive criticism and encouragement

To: Friend and neighbor Sherrell Weems Kmak

  For patiently sharing her computer skills

To: Publisher Vera Foster Rollo, PhD

  For faith that this book would do justice to its subject

TABLE OF CONTENTS

TABLE OF CONTENTS (Continued)

LIST OF ILLUSTRATIONS

FOREWORD

History is not always made up of earthshaking developments and larger-than-life heroes forging lengthy, dramatic and important chapters in the telling.

For history also is written by the lesser-known individuals, unsung and often obscure people playing roles in almost-forgotten events. They may not contribute entire chapters, but their deeds and experiences at the very least form tiny slivers of achievement that fit neatly into the vast mosaic of civilization's scientific progress. And nowhere is this more true than in the story of man's conquest of the skies.

The "around the rim flight" was a classic example of an aerial accomplishment that has been often ignored in the multi-volumes chronicling aviation's advances. I dare say that if the program *Do You Want to be a Millionaire* ever used "what was the around the rim flight?" as a million-dollar question, Regis Philbin would be lucky to find one person out of several hundred thousand who knows the right answer.

Miriam Seymour's exciting story of that gallant flight has to be read – and certainly more thoroughly enjoyed – in the context of the era in which it occurred: 1919.

The aircraft involved, called the Martin GMB and flown by men of the infant Army Air Service, was the prototype of America's first heavy bomber and as such was the great-grandfather of the legendary big warbirds that followed – the B-17, B-24, B-29, B-47 and B-52, all the way up to and including the B-2 Stealth.

The distance between the GMB and its descendents can be likened to the distance between the Neanderthal Man and a rocket scientist, yet that is the significance, not to mention the pure pleasure to be derived from Seymour's book. It comes at a time when the nation is preparing to celebrate the 100th anniversary of the first powered heavier-than-air flight at Kitty Hawk, North Carolina, December 17, 1903. The GMB, a biplane with two basically untested engines plus the built-in headwinds of struts and wires, technically wasn't that much different from the immortal Wright Flyer except in size.

Both airplanes were among the winged machines that made the early clumsy steps toward aviation's future and at a time when aircraft like Boeing's B-52 and 747 were mere scientific fiction fantasies. Who could have foreseen that only a century after Kitty Hawk, a mere heartbeat in history, the length of a 747 fuselage would be longer than the distance the Wright Flyer covered on its first flight? Or that less than 72 years after the rim flight demonstrated air power's potential in a primitive biplane (its range was a very theoretical and optimistic 824 miles with a cruising speed of only 92 mph), the B-2 would be flying at supersonic speeds nonstop from its U.S. base into the Gulf War zone?

My friend and fellow aviation historian Miriam Seymour, has expressed her gratitude to me for writing this foreword. It wasn't necessary. One doesn't need thanks for an assignment that was more of a privilege. This is an exemplary job of story-telling blended with scrupulous research, especially appropriate in the current atmosphere of criticism toward civil and military aviation alike. In effect, she turns our eyes toward the past so we can look at the present with awed appreciation for what has transpired in so short a time.

So I can only offer the supreme accolade of one author to another: I wish I had written it myself.

> Robert J. Serling
> Former Aviation Editor
> United Press International

ACKNOWLEDGEMENTS

It would be my great pleasure to include the name of every person who has helped me as I reached for the point where I could write this story. That's not possible for the very simple reason that if I listed all the names of all the people whose camaraderie and conversations I've enjoyed over the years, there would not be enough pages left to tell the story of *The Around The Rim Flight*.

As a substitute I offer this expression of gratitude and thanks from the heart -

To all the folks who were around Chicago airports named Sky Harbor, PalWaukee, Chicagoland, Midway and O'Hare, in the '50s and '60s.

To everyone I had the privilege of working with in the Aviation and Aerospace Industry in the State of Florida between 1970 and 1993.

To the good people who were part of FAA and trade associations including, but by no means limited to, AAHS, AOPA, AWA, FAMA, FATA, NATA and NBAA.

To all the librarians, researchers, archivists, curators and protectors of things historic, for their invaluable help.

To my late husband, Francis P. "Ted" Seymour (ATP, DC-3, D-18, Lockheed Lodestar, B-25, Learjet Models 23 and 25) who set unmatchable standards of always-best performance during his 30 year career as a professional pilot flying corporate aircraft.

To all the valued friends who patiently read re-writes, and

To a Guardian Angel who kept alive a stubborn determination to tell this story of courage and accomplishments that will forever be part of every flight carrying humankind across earth's skies and beyond.

PROLOGUE

Every story has a time frame. It may be today, tomorrow or history.

The story you are about to read is history. The year is 1919.

World War I is over but wars continue. Finland is fighting against a Russian take-over. France and Syria are battling for territorial control. Great Britain fights to retain her foothold in Asia. Tribal wars and guerilla actions plague Africa and South America.

In the United States the public demands disarmament but President Woodrow Wilson works hard to promote his belief that there should be a League of Nations with power to end all wars and enforce peace throughout the world.

His idealistic views are overwhelmed by strident voices preaching isolationism and the assurance that the Atlantic and Pacific oceans, a few Navy ships and a limited Army, will provide all the protection the country needs. Congress agrees and says foreign involvement should be limited to the Western Hemisphere.

Army manpower is reduced from 2,395,742 in 1918 to 851,624 in 1919, turning loose more than a million men to exercise their rights to life, liberty and the pursuit of happiness. They will test the promise of a bright future in this age of jazz, automobiles and unrest.

Married couples eke out bare existence on an average income of $2,000.00 a year. Under such restricted financial circumstances the production of children is regarded as the height of social irresponsibility. Yet children are born and taken care of. There is pride and satisfaction in doing one's best under the worst of circumstances.

PROLOGUE – Continued

Education is emphasized. Correspondence schools offer hope with their learn-at-home-in-your-spare-time courses that will teach anyone how to become a great salesman, or an automobile mechanic, or a certified electrician.

In big cities electricity is replacing gas for home lighting. Electric motors power streetcars, elevated trains and subways. A rail system called The Interurban is an efficient and convenient way to travel between cities.

Horses still provide transportation for those who cannot afford $350 for one of Mr. Ford's automobiles. Horses also pull the wagons used for home deliveries of milk and blocks of ice, but getting horses off city streets is a priority. Horse droppings are recognized as a potential health hazard and removal is a constant problem for city sanitation crews.

Baseball is the most popular sport and every city, town and hamlet has at least one playing field. The Major and Minor Leagues operate on regular schedules and the charge that five players on the Chicago White Sox team conspired to throw the World Series does little to dampen enthusiasm for the national pastime.

Jack Dempsey takes the world heavyweight boxing crown from Jess Willard.

The world of thoroughbred racing is electrified when Sir Barton, with J. Loftus in the saddle, wins the Kentucky Derby, the Belmont Stakes and the Preakness. (It will be ten years before this is referred to as the Triple Crown.)

A Peugot racer wins the Indianapolis 500 at the breakneck speed of 88.1 miles an hour.

PROLOGUE – Continued

There are 1,651,625 registered automobiles and for the year 1919, Texaco claims sales of 258 million gallons of high test gasoline.

The State of Oregon imposes a tax on gasoline. The State of New York inaugurates written tests for driver license applicants and the City of Detroit installs the world's first traffic control light.

Long distance communication is the big growth industry. Telephone and telegraph companies have stretched some 394 million miles of wire across the country. A three-minute telephone call between New York and San Francisco costs $16.50.

Public demand for a telephone in the home is creating local switchboard companies. Connections are made manually. You lift the receiver on your home unit, a buzz sounds on the switchboard. The person working the board – usually a female addressed as "Central" – asks for the name of the person you want to talk to, then makes the connection. "Central" is one of the first industrial jobs offered to women.

Wireless communication is used by ships at sea but radio broadcasting as a way to convey information and entertainment has not yet evolved. Record players known as Victrolas play one record at a time. The hand-wound machines cost $300.00.   The electric models cost $365.00.

A new dance called The Shimmy is introduced and in San Francisco a gentleman named Paul Whiteman, who will soon introduce to the world a singer with the unlikely name of Bing Crosby, organizes his first jazz band.

Women's fashions go softly feminine and the rigid, confining corsets that for decades pinched and shaped the female form, are cheerfully discarded. There are those who say this will encourage immoral behavior.

PROLOGUE – Continued

Long distance travel is getting easier and safer. Trains pulled b
Increasingly powerful steam locomotives operate over 400,00
miles of track, moving people, produce and products from coast t
coast in only five days.

The public accepts this kind of speed on the ground as progres
but does not accept the idea that aeroplanes will one day compet
with railroads.

Pilots are heroes but the machines they fly are not to be trusted.

 In June Alcock and Brown fly non-stop across the Atlantic in 1
hours 12 minutes. Men who look to the future say this is proof tha
people will one day travel long distances by air. Skeptics scof
Their favorite saying: "If God wanted man to fly, He would hav
given him wings."

Answering that challenge by showing the country the peacetim
usefulness of aeroplanes, is the core idea that develops into
9,823-mile long flight paralleling the borders of the United States.

GLENN MARTIN BOMBER (GMB) OVER WASHINGTON, D.C.

Original photo from 1976 files of Martin-Marietta Company, Baltimore, Maryland

THE ORIGINAL CREW

Left to right:

Flight Commander Lieutenant Colonel R. S. Hartz

First Pilot First Lieutenant Lotha A. Smith

Assistant Pilot Second Lieutenant E. E. "Tiny" Harmon

Master Electrician Sergeant John "Jack" Harding, Jr.

Master Mechanic Sergeant Jarosla "Jerry" Dobias

Photo from Glenn L. Martin Company advertisement reproduced in Aeroplan Scrap Book Number 3, published by Northrup University Press, Inglewoo California © 1975

CHAPTER I

PRE – FLIGHT

July 24, 1919

Brigadier General William "Billy" Mitchell, Assistant to the Chief of the Army Air Service, frowns at the stack of papers on his desk and the overflowing IN box.

Whoever said an army travels on its stomach, he mutters to himself, never spent time at Air Service Headquarters, Bolling Field, Anacostia, D.C.

With a shrug he settles into the chair and picks up the paper on top of the nearest stack. It's a memorandum from Supply Section saying they cannot comply with his request to ship aviation oil to the Chamber of Commerce in Missoula, Montana. Shipping military supplies to a civilian agency is against Army regulations.

The General's impatience with red tape begins to frame a sarcastic response when the roar of powerful motors cuts through the morning silence. Dropping the offending memo and pushing back from the desk, he is out the door and striding across the grass to where a big biplane shimmers and shakes as her two 400hp Packard Liberty motors begin to warm up.

The aeroplane is officially Glenn Martin Bomber Number One (GMB). It is the first American designed and built medium bomber purchased by the Air Service.

Within the hour GMB, carrying a crew of five, will depart on a flight designed to test her strengths, define her weaknesses, and challenge the abilities and courage of her crew. The planned route

begins at Bolling Field, goes north to Augusta, Maine, west
Seattle, Washington, south along the Pacific Coast to San Dieg
California, turns east to New Orleans, Louisiana, goes around tl
Florida peninsula, then turns north again to follow the Atlantic Coa
back to Bolling Field.

Navigation aids will be automobile road maps, rivers, railroads ar
a magnetic compass.

Communications will be handled by telephone and telegra|
services. A request for radio gear has been turned down. Devic
for radio communication over land are still in the experimental sta(
and Army engineers are unwilling to risk the few pieces they ha'
by installing them in a new aeroplane about to embark on a perilo(
flight around the borders of the United States.

"Besides," the engineers ask, "who would you talk to? Nobody o
there has radios."

So GMB and her crew will fly above telephone and telegraph lin
to the nearest town, land in an open field and wait for a kind citiz(
to come by and give them a ride into town.

Weather forecasting for flyers has been suggested and the Na'
has made some progress. In response to the Army request for
long range forecast the Navy said, "Don't go. It's too late in tl
year. By the time you get to the Mississippi River, weather alor
the northern border will be into seasonal changes. Flyir
conditions across the Rocky Mountains will be marginal at best."

Information from the civilian National Weather Service operated I
the Department of Agriculture is strictly for farmers and or
considered good within a 100-mile radius. But it's all tha(
available on a daily basis.

Finding places to land is not a major concern. Any relatively smooth field large enough to accommodate the aeroplane will do. In the eastern part of the country there are landing fields prepared to accommodate air mail deliveries and there are a few fields for civilian flyers where all flyers are welcome.

Several cities claim to have "Aeroplane Landing Fields" but they must be used with care. As a rule they are part of multiple use land areas that include fairgrounds, race tracks and recreational facilities. Many military reservations have parade grounds or open areas that can be used as landing fields. This will be especially important west of the Mississippi River.

Fuel services and repair facilities are rare. Providers of high test automobile gasoline see no future in setting up businesses at landing fields. Fuel is delivered in drums and it's up to the flyers to pour the liquid through chamois or some other fabric capable of straining out impurities.

All these logistics flip through General's Mitchell's mind as he joins Rim Flight Commander Lieutenant Colonel R. S. Hartz who is standing in front of GMB. They exchange perfunctory salutes but don't try to talk over the motor noise. Practically everything has been said anyway. For the past several months these two men have plotted and planned and connived to get permission and money to make this flight.

Although opposites in temperament, they share the view that machines like GMB are the future of air transportation. A successful long distance flight will do much to prove their beliefs.

If the General had had his way, back when they first began to consider the idea of extended testing of GMB and her motors under less than ideal conditions, he would have issued orders for the flight to be made. But the Colonel pointed out that Congress was cutting back all appropriations for military aviation and any undertaking r properly described and officially sanctioned by the War Departme would have little chance of being funded.

"What do you suggest instead?" the general asked and the color replied, "I suggest that we submit a formal memo laying out sor very good reasons for making the flight and submit it throu normal channels."

The general frowned, then nodded. Col. Hartz had a reputation doing the impossible. "You write the memo, I'll approve it a personally hand it to General Menoher."

Col. Hartz smiled. This was his kind of challenge. During 18 yea of military service, he had become an expert at twisting red ta and bending rules to get what he wanted.

He knew there were several special flights being set up during tl year. Some were to lay out routes for air mail planes. Some we races to determine how long aeroplanes and flyers could rema aloft. The challenge, then, was to develop persuasive reasons fo flight that could circumnavigate the United States. His memo wou lay out those reasons, in detail, as five Missions.

First Mission: test the performance of the 400hp Liberty Motors ai assess how well they work in pairs.

Second Mission: test the durability of the aeroplane and its par under less than ideal operating conditions and with minimu maintenance.

Third Mission: show the aeroplane in communities where i aeroplane had gone before and explain how machines such a GMB will one day connect small towns to the rest of the country.

Fourth Mission: encourage communities to build landing fields and air ports using designs provided by the Army Air Service and thereby establish a safe air route around the perimeter of the United States.

The Fifth Mission was not spelled out in detail but it was clearly implied. The crew would act as recruiters for the Army Air Service and quietly bring to the attention of the public the importance of adequate appropriations for aeronautical development and the building of machines capable of serving as the country's first line of defense.

Additional paragraphs emphasized the importance and efficiency of aerial observations of parts of the country still unexplored. Such observations could plot resources and develop information for control and use of federal lands

Col. Hartz also named the men he felt would be an outstanding crew.

There was no mention of costs.

General Mitchell chuckled over all the details, scrawled "Recommend Approval, Wm. Mitchell" on the last page and bucked it into official channels.

Confident of an affirmative response, he immediately issued travel and transfer requests for the men named as crew and ordered GMB flown from the Engineering Test Station at McCook Field in Dayton, Ohio to Bolling Field. His next move was a Directive naming Col. Hartz as Commander of the "flight to circumnavigate the United States".

If someone had asked why he chose the Colonel, who was a low time pilot with only a Junior Military Airman (JMA) rating, to take charge of this sophisticated aeroplane, the General would probably have told a story well known among the men stationed at Bolling.

Col. Hartz had been assigned to Bolling to take charge of Field Operations and Flight Training. One of his first changes in training routines was to select the best of the fighter pilots and form them into a group he called The Army Air Service Flight Demonstration Team. Their purpose: show off the 94-mile-an-hour DH-4 and Army aviator flying skills at every public event they could get to.

During one of the frequent parades along Pennsylvania Avenue, in Washington, D.C., the Colonel led his Team down the Avenue at treetop level. After the flight a reporter asked, "Wasn't that dangerous?" and one of the pilots answered, "If Col. Hartz led us through the gates of hell, we'd follow."

Standing in front of the GMB watching the men go through pre-flight routines, the General can't help wondering what gates of hell are ahead for GMB and her crew.

Crossing the Allegheny Mountains is still a hazardous undertaking. Their planned route will take them across vast stretches of unexplored territory. They will be flying among and across the virtually unknown ranges of the Rocky Mountains. If anything goes wrong, GMB and her crew might never be found.

"On the other hand," the voice in his mind argues, "if all goes well their success will influence the future development of air travel."

While the General argues with himself over the possible fate of the venture, the two men who will do most of the flying sit in the control pit going through warm-up procedures for the Liberty motors.

First Lieutenant Lotha A. Smith, Reserve Military Aviator (RMA), Aeronautical Service, Army (ASA), is First Pilot. He knows GMB better than anybody, having been part of the team that put her through Engineering Testing at McCook Field. He makes no secret of his ambition to build a solid career in the Air Service. Whatever he does he does well and strictly by the book.

Assistant Pilot, Second Lieutenant Ernest E. "Tiny" Harmon, RMA, was once characterized as a careful barnstormer. He has never met an aeroplane he couldn't fly or teach others to fly. His philosophy of flying and living, is simple and uncomplicated. "Let's get on with it."

They are both big men, the control pit is small, and wearing bulky flying suits, there is little space for stretching or moving around. There is no heat and no protection from the elements, but openings in the floor will allow water to drain out when they fly through rain. The only concession to pilot comfort is a new device made up of a rubber hose with one end fastened over a hole in the floor. It is politely referred to as the pilot relief tube.

The pilots face a panel of 12 instruments: a wind-up clock (wound and set), altimeter, airspeed indicator, air temperature thermometer, fore and aft inclinometers (attitude indicators) and two each coolant temperature gauges, tachometers and oil pressure indicators.

Harmon stretches to check the fuel gauges and the magnetic compass mounted on the fuselage ahead of the tiny windshield. He notes that the compass-correcting magnets are fastened into their slots with paper tape.

"Should get that changed to waterproof tape before we leave," he says but as preparations move forward, it slips his mind.

Meantime off duty airmen gather to look over the big ship, ask questions, offer any help that might be needed, and follow the two Sergeants as they do a walk-around inspection of the outside of the aeroplane.

DIAGRAM OF GMB

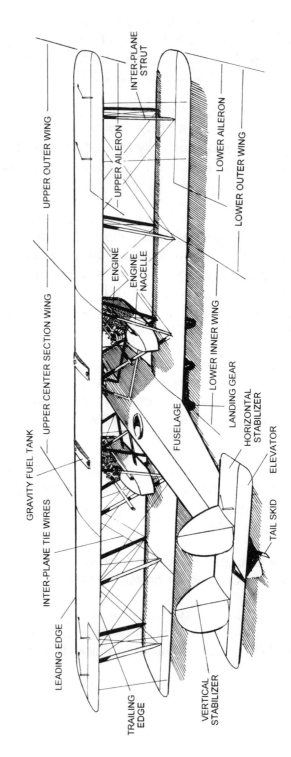

LEADING EDGE

TRAILING EDGE

INTER-PLANE TIE WIRES

GRAVITY FUEL TANK

UPPER CENTER SECTION WING

UPPER OUTER WING

INTER-PLANE STRUT

UPPER AILERON

ENGINE

ENGINE NACELLE

LOWER AILERON

LOWER OUTER WING

LOWER INNER WING

FUSELAGE

LANDING GEAR

HORIZONTAL STABILIZER

VERTICAL STABILIZER

ELEVATOR

TAIL SKID

Original drawing by artist Herbert C. Greif, Tucson, Arizona

Master Electrician Sergeant John "Jack" Harding moves to starboard and Master Mechanic Sergeant Jaraslov "Jerry" Dobias moves to the port side. Each of them has a clipboard and formal check list.

Motors: no gasoline or oil leaks.

Radiators: no signs of water leaking.

Gas tanks: full

Upper and lower wings: leading edge fabric smooth and well varnished.

Interplane ties: a quick pull and release of the wires produces a "thrum" that says they are as taut as they should be.

Interplane struts: no flaking paint. All fittings properly snugged down.

Moving around to the back of the wings, they check upper and lower ailerons: all hang level and move freely. Control cables inside the wings had been checked earlier in the week.

Walking slowly aft, both men run their hands along the fuselage, checking that fabric overlaps are varnished down tight. They bend down to examine belly fabric and make sure it's clean. Dirty fabric deteriorates quickly.

At the rear of the 72-foot-long fuselage they meet, check to be sure elevators and vertical fins move freely, and that bolts holding the tail skid are tight.

"Everything's okay on my side," Dobias says and Harding nods. "Cargo hold next."

Amidships on the port side they unlatch a door and Dobias steps up into the hold, calling off contents: 300 pounds of baggage, 1,200 pounds of gasoline in drums, 80 pounds of water, 72 pounds of aviation oil, 500 pounds of tools and spare parts and one set of four new tires.

Harding adds it up. "We're 1,152 pounds over the weight limit."

"Better not tell Lt. Smith," Dobias says. "He'll make us unload some of this stuff and I got a hunch we're gonna need every bit of it."

They close and latch the cargo door and move forward to finish their inspections with an examination of the rowboat shaped metal nose. All fittings and fastenings are secure.

Together they approach and salute General Mitchell and Colonel Hartz.

The Liberty motors shut down and the silence is momentarily deafening. Harding reports: "We are 1,152 pounds over our weight limit, Colonel."

Hartz nods. "Anything we don't need?" and when Harding says "No sir", Hartz replies, "We'll hope for the best."

Lts. Smith and Harmon join the group, salute, and Lt. Smith, standing stiffly at attention, reports: "All ready, Sir."

General Mitchell shakes hands with each of the crew, says a heartfelt "Godspeed" and with characteristic abruptness turns and strides back toward the Headquarters building. Everybody at Bolling Field knows GMB is leaving today. Nobody has asked when she will be back.

Colonel Hartz gives the word. "Let's go. First stop is Hazelhurst Station on Long Island. Do you have maps?"

Lt. Harmon answers, "I've flown that trip so many times I could do it in my sleep."

Lt. Smith frowns but the Colonel responds quietly, "Try to stay awake this time."

He walks over to the aeroplane and climbs into the forward gunner pit cut into the top of the metal nose. It is the least protected, most uncomfortable seat in the machine but it's the best for observing terrain.

The pilots resume their seats in the control pit, the sergeants move into position to swing the big propellers and the Libertys roar back to life.

Lt. Smith gives the "okay" sign and Harding and Dobias walk quickly around the port side, step onto the lower wing, swing onto the top of the fuselage and hold onto the railing between control pit and rear gunner pit as they make their way to their seats in the pit behind the trailing edge of the wing. It's a good vantage point for keeping an eye on the motors. Like the control pit and the forward gunner pit it has no overhead protection from the elements and no heat. There are the usual drain holes to prevent water accumulation but when there's no water, the drain holes suck in cold air.

It won't be comfortable flying, but flying is not a matter of comfort in this, the year 1919. Cold air at higher altitudes, rain, cruel winds and a host of other miseries are accepted as things to be endured.

GMB and her crew are ready to begin a journey that will test to levels unimagined, the motors, the machine and the men.

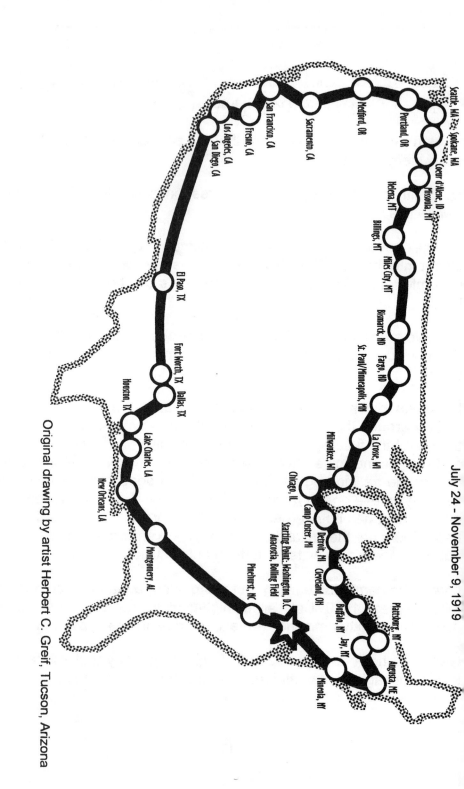

July 24 - November 9, 1919

Seattle, WA
Spokane, WA
Coeur d'Alene, ID
Missoula, MT
Portland, OR
Medford, OR
Sacramento, CA
San Francisco, CA
Fresno, CA
Los Angeles, CA
San Diego, CA
Helena, MT
Billings, MT
Miles City, MT
Bismarck, ND
Fargo, ND
St. Paul/Minneapolis, MN
La Crosse, WI
Milwaukee, WI
Chicago, IL
Camp Custer, MI
Detroit, MI
Cleveland, OH
Buffalo, NY
Jay, NY
Plattsburg, NY
Augusta, ME
Mineola, NY
Starting Point, Washington, D.C.
Anacostia, Bolling Field
Pinehurst, NC
Montgomery, AL
New Orleans, LA
Lake Charles, LA
Houston, TX
Dallas, TX
Fort Worth, TX
El Paso, TX

Original drawing by artist Herbert C. Greif, Tucson, Arizona

CHAPTER II

TAKE OFF AND TROUBLE

July 24

Satisfied that the motors are working well, Lt. Smith gives the sign and airmen who have come to watch the departure release the mooring ropes. GMB moves forward slowly. And sinks into a mud hole.

Two weeks of steady rain have turned parts of Bolling Field into a sea of mud and GMB is heavily loaded. Twenty men and both motors finally break her free and move her onto comparatively solid ground. The departure run is smooth and GMB does a slow, steady climb to 5,000 feet.

Half an hour later, over Baltimore, Dobias spots fluids leaking from the port motor. He nudges Harding, points to the problem, and lifts himself out of the gunner pit. Grasping the hand rail as an anchor against the powerful blast of the air stream, he inches forward and taps Lt. Smith on the shoulder. Looking rearward from the control pit, the leaks are easy to see.

Lt. Smith points downward but Dobias shakes his head. Checking to be sure a monkey wrench and a screwdriver are shoved deep into a pocket, he grabs hold of a vertical strut, puts one foot on each of the two support struts, and inches his way along until he reaches the motor. Gasping in the fierce stream of cold air that threatens to blow him off his precarious perch, he turns his back to the blast. With a clear and close-up view of the problems he sees that one leak is oil, the other water. Apparently the vibrations set up by the straining motors pulling GMB out of the mud at Bolling Field, had loosened the connections.

With his left arm hooked around the motor mount, he works the wrench out of his pocket, flexes fingers stiff with cold, and manages to tighten the loosened fittings. He hangs on long enough to be sure the leaks have stopped, then slowly makes his way back to his seat.

REPAIRS ABOVE THE GROUND

Original sketch by William D. Feeny, from in his book titled IN THEIR HONOR
© 1991, William D. Feeny

Shaking with cold, but with a satisfied grin on his face, he tells Harding , "Next time it's your turn."

Next time is five minutes later.

Responding to frantic signals from Lt. Harmon, Harding moves forward. Harmon has tried to make use of the pilot relief tube. Unfortunately the people who installed the tube did not understand the forces of suction and he's in dire danger of being unmanned. Harding hauls out his pocket knife and slashes the offending tube.

There are no more incidents and slightly less than three hours after departing Bolling Field, GMB drags her tail skid across the landing area at Hazelhurst Air Mail Station, Mineola, Long Island, New York.

CHAPTER III

NORTH TO AUGUSTA

July 24 and 25

The ground crew at Hazelhurst is glad to see GMB again. She had visited them often during the months she was in the testing program at McCook Field.

Willing hands help Harding and Dobias clean the dirt off the undersides of wings and belly, inspect the fuselage, tires and landing gear, and check liquids. It's all part of the routine that must be followed at the end of every flight. Gasoline is delivered to the aeroplane in drums on the back of a truck and a hand-operated pump lifts the fluid to the tanks on top of the wing. Every drop has to be filtered.

The auxiliary water reservoir has sprung a leak. With the help of one of the Hazelhurst mechanics, Harding and Dobias find what they need to make repairs and finish the job at dusk. Water must also be poured through a strainer to remove impurities. It all takes time but in the morning they'll be able to see at a glance if the leak has been stopped.

Harding leaves the radiator filling to Dobias and adds the oil he's requisitioned from the stores at Hazelhurst. Both men agree they will not use the oil they have on board unless it's absolutely necessary. Aviation oil is not a common product and there will be times, during the days ahead, when the oil will not be available from an outside source.

Meantime Hartz, Smith and Harmon confer with one of the air mail pilots as they plan the next leg of the flight.

- 17 -

"Augusta's easy to find," he tells them. "Follow the railroad tracks along the north shore to the end of Long Island, then turn north. Expect headwinds but otherwise the weather should be pretty good. The landing field at Augusta is on the southwest side of town."

Good food, good beds and good company, make overnight a pleasure and at 8:50 on Friday morning GMB heads north. Winds on the nose at 3,000 feet reduce ground speed to 81 miles an hour, allowing Col. Hartz ample time to make notes in the flight record book.

"Over East Greenwich at 10:02. Fields here have many stones in them. Race track southwest of Providence, Rhode Island is an excellent field with a good approach. Franklin Field at Boston is a good field. At Hamilton there is a good landing field three miles west of town." Farther north he notes: "a lot of pasture land. Would make excellent fields but cattle must be avoided."

Flying time to Augusta is four hours and 46 minutes and Lt. Smith guides GMB to the landing field southwest of town. Machine and crew take a beating as they bounce across the rough and rutted ground that has been marked as their landing area.

Harding, Dobias and Harmon do careful inspections of all the exterior fittings. There's no apparent damage.

The Adjutant General of the State of Maine, the governor's secretary, the Mayor of Augusta, and other officials form a greeting committee. An automobile is provided and men from the Police Department and the National Guard volunteer to guard GMB.

Col. Hartz expresses his appreciation. "If we get one-tenth such good care at all our stops, the trip will be both a pleasure and a success."

In return for the warm reception, some of the more prominent citizens are taken for a ride in GMB. They are impressed but the idea of setting aside perfectly good land and spending money to turn it into a place just for aeroplanes that might – or might not - land there at some future time doesn't fit into the pattern of Yankee thrift.

Hospitality extends through an excellent dinner and it is late when the crew is finally allowed to retire.

CHAPTER IV

WEATHER AND WOE

July 26

The destination today is Montpelier, Vermont. It is about 200 miles, to the west, which is the accepted standard for maximum distance between landing fields.

Col. Hartz tells the crew, "Before we leave Augusta let's see what the Weather Service at the Department of Agriculture has to say." and sends a wire asking for information about weather conditions over the states of New Hampshire and Vermont.

Weather Service wires back that there will probably be light rain over the White Mountains in eastern New Hampshire.

Smith and Harmon go over Rand McNally state maps that show roads, rivers, railroads and towns but have no information about the heights of the White Mountains or the Green Mountains in Vermont.

Lt. Harmon says, "If the weather's clear, we'll be able to see the mountains." and Lt. Smith snaps, "If the weather is bad, we will land and wait until it clears."

Col. Hartz introduces a newspaper reporter and asks Lt. Smith to take the man for a short hop. Another run across the dangerously bumpy field makes Harding and Dobias nervous. After the reporter departs, they again do a careful inspection.

Dobias shakes his head. "I don't like it. I got a feeling we're missing something."

Harding agrees. "We've been over the machine twice and haven't found any sign of damage. We can tell the Colonel what we think, but without something positive, he's going to say we go on."

At 11:15, with an audience of two boys who have sneaked away from school , GMB rumbles across the field, lifts, dips dangerously over the edge of the cliff at the end of the departure area, staggers a bit, rights herself, and begins to climb.

Harmon circles the town of Augusta, watching the temperature gauge on the right motor. It had been running high during the earlier flight, but now it's back within normal range. Satisfied that all is well, he turns GMB to a westward heading.

At 5,000 feet there are strong headwinds but the air is smooth enough for Col. Hartz to make notes in the flight record book: "we passed over first mountains range at 12:15 PM. There are no fields of any kind below.   No sign of railroads, houses, roads or anything but lakes, forests and rocks."

Fifteen minutes later GMB encounters the first storm.   Winds increase. Rain slams down, beating on men and machine, heavy and cold. Every flying minute is a fight to maintain control as GMB corkscrews in the switching, swirling winds.

Somehow Harmon keeps them on course and they reach Montpelier at 1:25. The worst of the storm has passed, but winds are still too strong to allow a landing.

Communicating by hand signals Col. Hartz and the pilots agree to continue flying west.   At 2:02 they cross over the south end of Lake Champlain, and identify the town of Essex, New York. They have been in the air three hours and ten minutes but Lt. Smith calculates there is sufficient gasoline to reach the vicinity of Buffalo where they will have a choice of good landing fields.

Another pile of mountains lies ahead. The country below is totally inhospitable. Clouds are closing in again. Light rain strengthens into a solid wall of water and elevators of air carry GMB up one minute and down the next with mind-numbing speed.

Smith and Harmon watch in helpless horror as the paper tape holding the compass-correcting magnets in place disintegrates and the magnets fall out, sliding slowly down the side of the fuselage. The compass is useless.

A break in the clouds provides a quick a look at the terrain. It's all mountains. But which mountains? If they are as far west as their time in the air indicates, they are over the Adirondacks. But the maps are impossible to unfold in the high winds and the strength of the winds has slowed their progress in whatever direction they may be traveling.

To continue with any degree of safety, they climb again and get high enough to be reasonably sure they are above the mountaintops. Holding hard on the controls, fighting the winds that switch direction from one moment to the next, rocking and rolling GMB until she is almost uncontrollable, Smith and Harmon manage to guide her through the bottom layer of clouds. There is another layer above, but the air is calmer and GMB settles down to smoother flying.

The altimeter reads 12,000 feet. The air is so cold it is impossible to take a deep breath and the right motor is acting up again.

The bone-freezing cold penetrates fur-lined flying suits. Their feet are numb. Gloves cannot keep their hands warm and the goggles they wear to protect their eyes, must come off before they freeze onto their skin. This is the worst of all the hardships. Without the protection of goggles eyesight can be badly damaged.

There is no choice but to stay between layers and hope. If a motor stops, or if they run out of fuel, it will be the end. The longer they can stay in the air, the better their chances of getting beyond the mountains into an area where there will be a place large enough to make a safe landing.

In the rear gunner's pit Dobias and Harding duck down behind the cowling where they can hear each other talk and assess the possible reasons for the problem with the motor. A closer look would be a good idea. They reach up, grasp the rail on top of the fuselage, and scan the motor. There's oil spewing out and it could be coming from the cam shaft. There may be a way to tighten up the protective covering.

Dobias moves forward, lowers himself slowly over the side until his feet touch the bottom wing, grabs a firm hold on cross-bars, and makes his way out to the laboring motor. As they suspected, the problem centers on the cam shaft . He turns and nods to Harding who passes him a hammer and chisel. With nearly frozen fingers, he manages to make some adjustments and turns back toward the fuselage, battling the strength of the air stream every step of the way.

His whole body is shaking and his eyes feel as if they are frozen, as he returns to the gunner pit and huddles down to give his body a chance to recover from the blasting, enervating cold.

The others shake their heads in awe. This is the second time Dobias has risked his life to save them.

The motor is running better and there is a break in the cloud deck below. Harmon dives down. Below the clouds they can see an open space that looks large enough for a safe landing.

On closer examination it is not suitable, but they are no longer over mountains and visibility is good. It's late afternoon and patches of mist are forming along a river but Harmon stays low. All eyes scan the ground.

There are a number of open spaces ahead. The first one is too small. The next one has too many trees. Another field up ahead looks good and whatever its size and condition, they must land. Gasoline gauges are reading empty.

Harmon takes GMB lower and lower for a good look at the big open area. It's a farm field planted in oats. Ground mists are spreading and there's no time to search for a better spot.

The crew applauds as he sets GMB down in a perfect landing but joy is short-lived. GMB swerves, digs a wing into the ground, snaps into a short, violent turn, and slams forward to stop with her nose half buried in the soggy ground and her tail in the air.

Impact sends Lt. Harmon flying out of his seat and over the front gunner pit where Col. Hartz is still seated. The Col. reaches up and with great good luck manages to grab hold of Harmon's coat collar. Harmon does a half-gainer and lands on his feet, unhurt.

The Colonel and both Sergeants extricate themselves from the wreckage, shaken but not injured.

Lt. Smith is the only casualty. His ankle is caught between bent bracing rods in the control pit and there is no way he can be freed until the tail of the aeroplane is brought down to ground level.

TAIL IN THE AIR, NOSE IN THE GROUND

Photo courtesy the Merle C. Olmsted Collection

A voice from the other side of the machine calls out, "You fellers need some help?"

It's Martin Howard, who owns the farm where GMB has come to rest. He and a neighbor heard the aeroplane, watched the approach and witnessed the crash.

Colonel Hartz turns to Harding and Dobias. "What do we do first?"

Harding responds. "Pull the tail down so we can see about Lt. Smith. After that we'll look at the wheels. If they're as bent up as I think they must be, we'll need logs to shove underneath to prop her up to as near level as we can manage. Then we can get the tools we need out of the cargo area and free Lt. Smith. But we'll need ropes to pull the tail down".

Farmer Howard nods, trots off to the nearby barn, returns in minutes with lengths of rope, a pair of ladders, and more neighbors.

One of them looks over the wreck, then turns to Dobias with a sly kind of smile says, "Think you can fix it?"

"Yes sir," Dobias snaps back. "And we'll save you a front row seat for when we fly her out."

The Colonel eyes Dobias for a spit second, then relaxes. "Before that day comes," he says calmly, "we have a few things to do. So let's get that tail lowered, get Lt. Smith out, secure everything as best we can, set up camp and have a meal."

Farmer Howard points across the field. "That house over there is empty. It's where my hired man and his family will live but they won't be moving in for another month. You can use it and my wife and the neighbor ladies will do your cooking and cleaning."

It's almost too good to be true. Tough Army men they may be but living in makeshift shelters and working outside in all kinds of weather is not a pleasing prospect.

Dobias sets a ladder against the fuselage next to the door to the cargo compartment. He ties a rope around his waist, mounts the ladder, opens the door, swings off the ladder into the cargo compartment, works his way up through the fuselage cross-bracing, loops the rope around the tail skid supports, tosses both ends down through the small opening around the tail skid, braces himself and yells, "Let her down easy."

Hartz, Harmon, Harding and the farmers line up, fireman fashion, along the rope. Harding calls out "heave" and the line moves slowly backward, pulling hard to lift the nose cone out of the dirt. Slowly, then faster and faster, the tail comes down, slams into the ground, bounces once, and GMB is back in three-point position.

Dobias releases the rope from the inside, makes his way back out and down to the ground rubbing a shoulder and asks Col. Hartz, "Do we get medals for bruises?"

Harding hauls tools out of the cargo compartment, selects a wrench, steps onto the lower wing, and climbs into the control pit beside Lt. Smith. In a matter of minutes the bent bars are spread and the Lt. manages to step over the side of the control pit onto the wing. He lowers himself to sitting position and slides off onto the ground, standing on one foot. He can't put any weight on the injured ankle.

With Lt. Harmon on one side and Farmer Howard on the other, he hops across the field to the farm house while Col. Hartz and the sergeants dig out all the pieces of canvas they have in the cargo hold.

Farmer Howard has pinpointed some dead trees for shoring up the fuselage. Spectators help move them over to the aeroplane, and as the mists thicken, crewmen and farmers work together to shove the logs in place, cover the damaged areas with canvas and tie GMB down for the night.

The farmers say goodnight and Hartz, Harding and Dobias walk slowly across the field to the farmhouse.

After a wash-up, a change into dry clothing, and a hearty supper prepared by Mrs. Howard, Col. Hartz assigns duties.

"Sergeants, you have full responsibility for the aeroplane.

Lt. Harmon, you will handle visitors and assist the sergeants in whatever way you can.

Lt. Smith, you must stay off that ankle, so you'll be in charge of all the paper work.

I will be liaison between Headquarters, Supply Section, Engineering Service at McCook and the Martin factory in Cleveland.

Tonight let's get some rest and tomorrow morning we'll start planning. The name of the nearest town, by the way, is Jay, New York and we're 18 miles from Lake Champlain. That's about 50 miles north of where we first crossed the lake. During those two hours after the magnets fell out of the compass, and we were between the two layers of clouds, we were actually flying in a circle."

He pauses, then adds, "We must be five of the luckiest people in the world." There are nods all around and the Col. continues.

"I'll report our position to Headquarters but since today is Saturday there probably won't be any response until Monday.

Tomorrow morning at first light, we'll take a good look at the damage and start a list of what we need. Then first thing Monday morning I'll telegraph the lists to Supply Section and to the depot at McCook. After that's done I'll telephone Headquarters, report our position and circumstances and request another mechanic. Any other ideas or suggestions?"

"I believe you've covered everything," Lt. Smith says and the others nod their agreement.

"Good, We've been through enough today. Now let's turn in for a good night's rest. Tomorrow will be a tough day."

CHAPTER V

BENT BUT NOT BROKEN

July 27 through August 26

Dawn winds and rain showers accompany Harmon, Harding and Dobias as they walk across the field between farmhouse and aeroplane.

Harmon shakes his head. "Didn't look this bad last night." He turns to Dobias. "Yesterday you told one of the farmers she'd fly out of here. Do you really believe that?"

Dobias answers with quiet confidence. "Yessir, I do. It's a big job but we can handle it. "

Harding adds, "Some warm and dry weather will help. Looks like the toughest part of the job will be changing the nose.. This one's bent beyond repair. The Martin factory will have to send us a new one. Removing the damaged one is no problem but the three of us and the Colonel, can't lift the weight of a new nose and hold it in place long enough to fasten it down."

"Do you suppose somebody from the factory will come out and help?" Harmon asks. "And let's hope Headquarters approves the Colonel's request to send us another mechanic."

Harding nods. "We're going to need all the help we can get."

Farmer Howard joins them in time to hear Harding's last remark. "Me and my neighbors will help," he says. "And between the lot of us we can do woodworking and welding and brazing.

Our blacksmith's pretty good with all kinds of metal. And you can borrow any tools we have."

Lt. Harmon answers, "We appreciate that, Mr. Howard. And I'm sure we'll be asking."

Harding and Dobias add their thanks and Farmer Howard looks at the damaged machine, shakes his head. "Don't know how you're gonna do it," he says. "But I'm off to Sunday services and we'll include you boys in our prayers."

The three men resume their walk along the side of the aeroplane and as they approach the wings, Harding points to a broken strut still attached to the outside wheel of the landing gear. He hunkers down to examine the damage.

"Look at this," and points to a broken wheel support. "Somebody did a rotten job of brazing the joint that's supposed to hold the wheel support to the frame. It cracked from the inside out, and when this wheel went, the weight shifted to the second wheel and then to the third and fourth wheels. Both axles are too bent to be straightened. We'll have to get new wheels and new axles from the factory."

Harmon has walked back to trace their landing track. "It was still holding when we set down," he says. "See how the four wheels and the tail skid tracks are in a straight line? And here ... it's what .. about 15 feet ? You can see where the brazing actually let go and the crash happened." He rejoins Harding and Dobias. "What do we do next?"

Harding stands up. "Damage analysis. Let's get the clipboards and start a list of what needs to be done. Once we have that, we can decide about special tools and supplies to ask Supply Section for and what we have to order from the Martin factory."

"And Lt., we'll need some boards to lay on the ground when we start removing damaged parts. Would you take a look around and see what you can find?"

"On my way," Harmon says and moves off as Dobias returns with clipboards, ready to make notes as Harding describes damaged areas.

Landing gear, starboard side: struts for both wheels broken and pushed through lower wing. Both wheels and axle bent. Must be replaced. Same for gear on port side. Tires are ruined but we have four new ones in the cargo hold.

Metal stress rod under forward section of fuselage: Badly bent. Order new one from factory.

Wings, starboard side: wooden ribs broken and sticking up through fabric on both wings. Order ribs from factory.

Need to replace at least 50% of the fabric on all four wings. Order from factory and keep what we have in reserve. Same for varnish.

Aileron frame on starboard wing twisted and fabric ripped. Frame can be straightened but fabric must be replaced.

Rigging Wires and Support Struts: Wires broken. Replace with new wire. Metal struts between wings on both sides need to be straightened.

Motors and propellers: Appear to be undamaged.

Nose: Crushed. Order new one from Martin Factory.

Fuselage: 25% of fabric damaged.

Tail Section: Everything appears to be okay.

Harding puts down the pencil and rubs his eyes. "That's a start. Let's check out tool boxes and decide what special equipment we need to order from McCook. "

Dobias climbs into the cargo compartment. "One thing we don't have is welding equipment, but maybe we can use what the farmers have."

"We'll ask," Harding replies. Then adds,   "While you're in there, take a look at the control cables. See any damage?"

"Yeah, some breaks in the cables but they can be spliced. And a couple of the bracing rods have come loose. No major damage that I can see right now. Need better light to see if there's anything else.   Next time the sun comes out, I'll look again."

He jumps down to the ground and closes the cargo door.   "I'm hungry."

Harding   looks toward the farm house. "There's Mrs. Howard carrying a basket. Let's go see what she brought for breakfast."

During breakfast, Harding and Dobias make their report to Colonel Hartz and detailed planning gets under way. They will finish inspecting for damage inside and out, set up work space and begin removing damaged parts. Finding adequate canvas tarpaulins to protect everything from rain and wind will be a priority. Cutting out damaged fabric and patching in new material will have to wait until the weather clears. Rain is murder on bare fabric and varnish will not set up when humidity is high.

Maybe Farmer Howard has some extra canvas and tarpaulins they can borrow. Lt. Harmon will help when and where he can, but his primary responsibility is to handle visitors who are already coming to get a close-up look at an aeroplane.

Lt. Smith can begin setting up his work area in the house. There will be an enormous amount of record keeping, tracking orders for parts and parts received. He must also maintain a daily log to show work done, number of visitors, and any money spent in local stores.

Farmer Howard has agreed to drive the Colonel into town first thing Monday morning and introduce him to the telegraph operator and the telephone people. Headquarters needs to know exactly where they are, how they can be reached, and how material and supplies can be shipped in.

The Colonel will include all that in his report describing the condition of the aeroplane and their general situation and asking for another mechanic.

He'll also request travel orders for the train trip to the Martin factory in Cleveland to work with the Martin factory people as they fill the order for replacing structural members that can't be rebuilt in the open field. Replacing the metal nose will be their biggest problem.

" It may be several hours before Headquarters responds." he tells the crew. "But I'll buy any supplies Lt. Smith needs and get acquainted with the people in town. I think we should invite them to come out and see the machine so they know what we're doing. Some of them may have skills we can use."

Lt. Harmon interrupts and gestures toward the window. "Visitors already, " and heads for the door.

The rest of the afternoon is spent making detailed lists of equipment, supplies and new parts and outlining orderly plans for tackling an impossible job under far from ideal conditions.

<u>July 28, 29 and 30</u>

It's a gloomy Monday as the crew begins the job of putting GMB back together again.

Working in the open field, buffeted by winds rolling down the valley and chilled by intermittent showers, the sergeants use boards salvaged from a collapsed farm building to build work benches. A couple of dead tree trunks are trimmed, moved over and driven into the ground beside the work benches. Boards are laid across the tops to provide a platform that will keep damaged parts off the wet ground.

Eyeing the growing heap of broken pieces, Harding asks, "Which would you rather do, Jerry. Woodworking, metal working, cable splicing or fabric patching?"

Dobias retorts, "You mean I've got a choice?"

They laugh together, shrug and get on with doing one chore at a time.

It is late afternoon before all the damaged parts except the nose are removed. One of the farmers offers the use of what turns out to be a well-equipped workshop. The local blacksmith hauls away a load of bent metal parts, promising to have them straightened out and back in no time at all.

More tarpaulins have been found and everything is carefully covered as night falls. Harmon, Harding, and Dobias return to the farm house. Over a hearty meal they outline what they have done, and Colonel Hartz reports on what he has been able to accomplish.

Bad news first. Headquarters refuses to send another mechanic. Supply Section says it will complete paperwork as soon as possible but everything we are asking for has to be ordered from McCook. Supply says they can't promise delivery dates because they've no idea how long it will take to ship from Dayton, Ohio to Jay, New York.

The good news is approval of travel orders for Col. Hartz to go to Cleveland. He has purchased a ticket for the westbound train on Wednesday morning.

Tuesday morning the world looks much better. The sun is shining as the work of dismantling damaged sections goes on. Assessing what can be done with tools and materials on hand and how much can be done with the help of local farmers is the main project. Energy and enthusiasm work together to generate a cautious optimism that one day soon GMB will be ready to fly again.

Wednesday morning the skies are threatening more rain. The crew salutes as Col. Hartz departs to board the train for Cleveland. Lt. Smith has his work space set up in the farm house and begins writing reports of activities and plans.

Harmon, Harding and Dobias walk slowly through the light drizzle, discussing what can be done.

This is a good day to work inside the fuselage," Harding says and Dobias agrees, adding, "Let's move everything out of the cargo space, so we'll have room to lay out the cables and start splicing."

Contents of the cargo space are set under the fuselage and Harmon borrows a lantern to provide additional light. Damaged control cables are pulled. They need to be spliced in 29 places Harmon asks if they'll teach him how to do the work.

He and Harding sit on the floor of the cargo compartment while Dobias makes his way through the interior of the fuselage, marking places were fabric is damaged and replacing a pair of anchor bolts that hold cross-bracing rods in place.

By noon the weather clears and there are visitors, some from as far away as Montreal, Canada. .Lt. Harmon resumes his chores as host, answering questions and sneaking pieces of damaged fabric or metal to youngsters.

"Future pilots" he says. Harding and Dobias grin and assure him. "We didn't see you giving away government property. "

Young visitor gets a close-up look at the damage.

Photo courtesy the Merle C. Olmsted Collection

The work of identifying and salvaging useful parts takes up much of the afternoon. Not knowing what equipment and supplies will be shipped first or when they will arrive, makes any kind of planning difficult.

Little things are big problems.   Cotter pins, nuts, bolts, wood screws, and sealing rings are all in short supply.   Some substitutes are found in the local farm stores.   Ingenuity and improvisation create what can't be bought.

Tools and equipment are separated in order of use.   Motors, motor supports and propellers are carefully examined. They appear to be in good condition. Supporting framework will require some minor repairs but that can be done last.

In the evening Farmer Howard comes to the farmhouse with a telegram from McCook.   Half the requested supplies will arrive on Thursday, the 31st.

"That's tomorrow," Lt. Smith points out and asks Farmer Howard if he will arrange for a truck to pick up the crates at the railroad depot and deliver them to the aeroplane.

July 31

Sunshine brightens everybody's day. The first shipment of parts arrives in wood crates which are knocked apart so the boards can be used to build work benches and more storage space.

Setting ladders against the nose at the point where metal and fabric are connected,   Harding and Dobias check out fastenings that hold the nose cone in place.   Once they're loosened, the nose can be dropped to the ground.   Another dent won't make any difference. But the big question remains: how can the new nose be lifted into place.

VISITORS AND VOLUNTEERS.

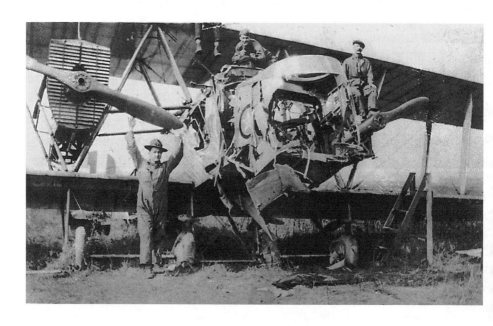

Photos courtesy the Merle C. Olmsted Collection

Colonel Hartz wires from Cleveland that he and two volunteers from the Martin factory will arrive on the sixth. They're bringing new wing ribs, landing gear, fabric and other assorted parts. The factory mechanics will stay as long as they are needed.

Maybe they will have some ideas about the nose," Dobias says.

A rain shower drives them under a piece of tarp and one of the farmers who is walking beside Dobias says, "You boys could use some protection out here. Maybe you should ask the railroad people to borrow their tent ."

"Good idea," Dobias agrees. "A small tent would be a big help."

"This is a big one," the farmer says. "There was this circus that came to town and couldn't pay its freight bill so the railroad took the tent. It's big enough to cover the whole aeroplane."

Lt. Harmon bums a ride into town, gets the railroad to agree to lend the tent and talks one of the local truckers into delivering it to the crash site. What a relief it will be to work under cover but having cover still doesn't solve the problem of removing and replacing the nose.

One of the visitors who has been listening to all the talk about the nose, steps forward. "Before you put up the tent, dig a pit. "

"A pit?"

"Sure. You gotta get that nose down to ground level. So dig a hole in the ground wide enough for the wings and deep enough so the bottom of the metal part touches the ground. Slope one side and

- 41 -

you can roll the machine down into the pit then use big rocks to hold it in place."

" But will Farmer Howard let us to dig up his field?"

Farmer Howard weighs the suggestion. He can stipulate that the hole be filled in, of course. But then he has a better idea. He smiles and says, "Go ahead. When you fellas fly outta here, it'll be a good swimming hole for the kids."

There are whoops of laughter and back-slapping congratulations all 'round.

August 6

Colonel Hartz and the Martin volunteers are startled when they see the circus tent lying on the ground and digging equipment at work in front of GMB.

An explanation of what's going on gets their enthusiastic endorsements and everybody pitches in to unload the truckload of supplies from the factory.

First job: landing gear repairs. New parts are laid out, tires are pulled out and fitted to new wheels, and as darkness falls, the last bolt slides into place. With careful precision the logs that have been supporting GMB are removed. She settles slowly onto her new gear.

August 7 and 8

Next big job: replace the stress bar under the fuselage where the metal nose is fastened to the fabric-covered framework. With the help and guidance of the factory men the replacement is quickly installed. GMB can now be moved with minimum effort.

The timing is exactly right. The pit is also finished and the ramp is graded.

A farm tractor hitched to the tail controls the rate of descent and GMB rolls gently down the ramp to stop with the damaged nose cone slightly above the top rim of the pit. She's in perfect position for the difficult job of removing the old nose and sliding on the new one.

Farmers and visitors pitch in to raise the tent and by mid-morning on Friday the men can work without worrying about weather.

Platforms are built in a semi-circle around the front of the machine and the Martin men begin the job of removing the nose. They will crate it and take it with them when they return to the factory.

A telegram arrives announcing that the new nose is ready for shipping and will arrive at Jay on the 18th.

With calm confidence that all problems are solved, Harmon, Dobias and Harding give the motors and propellers a casual check. A pair of visiting automobile mechanics are like kids in a toy shop when asked if they'd like to lend a hand.

"Wait 'til we get home and tell the folks how we helped build an aeroplane," they say. It will be something to brag about forever.

Dobias looks out at the blue summer sky and cracks, "Wouldn't you know? Now that we have shelter, the weather clears up."

Harding grins. "Way of the world, Jerry. Let's leave the motors for later and see if we can't finish patching and varnishing fabric. It would be nice to have that out of the way before we start on the nose."

August 9 through 16

Work gets done amid wisecracks and insults and occasional profanity. Someone wonders aloud about the condition of the motors. Until the tent went up, they were exposed to the elements. Will they fire up or will they have to be replaced?

Harding and Dobias refuse to speculate.

Each day ends with pride and frustration. Installing wing ribs takes time and patience. High humidity delays the fabric varnishing process.

Visitors are a blessing and a problem. Courtesy is a standing order. Lt. Harmon manages to keep people from interfering with the actual work, but when he can't answer questions, he doesn't hesitate to interrupt Harding or Dobias or the Martin men.

Each man is aware of their unspoken, but important, mission to build good will for the Army Air Service. The more the public learns about the aeroplane and its importance to the future of the country, the easier it will be to get Congress to appropriate money for military aeronautical development.

The men from Martin understand and help. Their future is also at stake. If GMB can complete this flight with a good performance record, there will be future orders to keep the factory going.

Failure of men, machine or motors is unthinkable.

August 17

Colonel Hartz decrees an easy day. Some clean-up work is done in preparation for the arrival of the new nose but mainly it's a day of relaxing and planning the next effort. Various theories are advanced as to how the heavy new nose can be lifted into position but in essence it all comes down to the need for brute strength.

The Martin men point out that the gas tanks should be removed before they try to slide the damaged nose off. Also it will be a good idea to check all fastenings to be sure they have everything they need to secure the new nose.

August 18, 19 and 20

The nose arrives and the crate is moved inside the tent while gas tanks are being removed. Taking them off is comparatively easy but before they can be re-installed, the supporting joists will have to be rebuilt.

"Nothing's simple," Dobias mutters as he concentrates on sorting damaged nuts and bolts and laying out replacements.

By noon on the 20th both tanks are off and the nose can be pushed off. With all the fasteners removed, the men work to push it away from the fuselage, It acquires some more dents as it finally drops to the ground. After the new nose is in place, the old one will be crated for shipping back to the factory.

August 21

This is the big day. Everything is ready for installing the new nose. A dozen farmers come in to help. Visitors volunteer.

Slowly, steadily, they lift the heavy shape, rest it on the lower step of the scaffolding, take deep breaths, lift again, tilting it backward just enough to allow holes around the bottom edge to slide over the bolts on the underside. Muscles strain as the men push the con up and forward. They work slowly and carefully, gradually workin the unwieldy thing over the bolts. One last heave and it settles int place.

It's a perfect fit.

Cheers echo across the tent. Perspiring faces gleam with pride. It' an experience none of them will ever forget.

August 22 and 23

Work now concentrates on snugging down the nose, rebuilding th support joists and getting the gas tanks back in place. Coppe tubing needs to be repaired before fuel lines are re-connected. It i slow, painstaking work but the job is completed as evening roll across the valley.

August 24

At breakfast Col Hartz raises a question: "Anybody remembe what day this is?"

There's no response and he continues, "This day last month w took off from Bolling Field."

Lt. Smith shakes his head. "And here we sit, not even a thousan miles logged. What can our chances be for completing the rest (this assignment?"

The colonel looks at each face around the table. He sees two ver good pilots and four superb mechanics who have worked miracle during the past month. Quietly he answers Lt. Smith. "I'd say on hundred percent."

Okay, you guys, you heard the Colonel. Let's get a move on." Lt. Harmon says as he heads for the door.

This is a day for doing odds and ends. Tools are collected and sorted. Borrowed items are returned with thanks and the wooden work benches and scaffolding are given to the farmers. The crated nose cone is loaded onto a truck and the Martin men are driven to the railroad station for their trip back to Cleveland.

Harding and Dobias go through piles of stuff, salvage whatever they may have future use for and leave the rest for anyone who wants it.

Over at the farmhouse Lt. Smith is completing his records and boxing up the paperwork.

Col. Hartz and Lt. Harmon walk the length of the field, marking the smoothest part for the departure run.

August 25 and 26

Morning sunshine bounces off her new nose as Farmer Howard's tractor pulls GMB up the ramp and out of the pit. As soon as the aeroplane is out in the open the tent is knocked down and folded for return to the railroad warehouse.

Dobias and Harding inspect fabric repairs and add another coat of varnish. New magnets are inserted and a transit is borrowed to true up the compass. Tools and salvaged materials are packed up and loaded into the cargo compartment which will remain open until Lt. Smith finishes packing the records he's kept for the past month.

The usual hubbub of conversation is subdued. Work is done with quiet efficiency. It's almost as if there are regrets that the end of a challenging job is in sight.

The stillness is shattered by the roar of motors and Lt. Smith limps to the doorway of the farmhouse to stare in amazement at the whirling propellers. Later he learns that both motors fired on the first pull of the props.

It's a big plus for the mission to test the capabilities of the Liberty motors. Starting up as they have is a good indication that they will operate dependably under less than perfect conditions. Sitting unprotected through wind and rain and the normal dirt of out-of doors has not affected their ability to fire and fly.

Tuesday is final clean-up for aeroplane, field and farmhouse. With what they feel are inadequate expressions of thanks, the crew say farewell to all the good folks who have done so much to get GMB ready to fly again.

Col. Hartz goes into town and sends a wire direct to General Menoher: "We resume flight tomorrow morning. Will stop at Plattsburg Barracks for gasoline and oil."

<u>August 27</u>

Lt. Smith's ankle is still painful but he manages to climb into the control pit beside Lt. Harmon. Col. Hartz takes his seat in the forward gunner pit in the new nose. Harding and Dobias swing the propellers and scramble back to their seats.

Lt. Harmon turns GMB into the wind, guides her slowly to the part of the field he'd marked for the departure run, takes a deep breath and applies power. She lumbers forward, slowly gathering speed, struggles into the air, climbs to 500 feet, circles, dips her wings to the waving, cheering crowd, and turns north to follow the valley of the Au Sable River to the military base named Plattsburg Barracks.

It's a 14-minute flight and the parade ground at the Barracks is more than adequate for a safe landing. Off-duty personnel surround the crew, firing questions, helping secure the big machine. In record time GMB is moored, tires and landing wheels are inspected, a couple bolts are tightened, gasoline and oil are added and the water radiators are checked and filled.

GMB and her crew are ready for whatever tomorrow may bring.

CHAPTER VI

UP, UP AND AWAY - AGAIN

August 28 through September 2

Officers and enlisted men at Plattsburgh Barracks are fascinated by GMB. It's the first opportunity they've had to examine a big aeroplane. They get in everybody's way in their efforts to make the crew feel welcome.

Col. Hartz and Lt. Harmon take the Commandant, several officers and helpful enlisted men for rides. They don't mention that the short hops are also test flights to make sure GMB is performing satisfactorily.

As a result of the aerial view of the Barracks, the Commandant has a better understanding of the idea that landing field markings should be the same for all Army Air Service facilities. Col. Hartz does a quick sketch to show where markings should be placed and has Harding and Dobias prepare the list of supplies needed. The two of them spend the next day working with Barracks personnel, checking out supplies in the storage room. Everything is jammed together in no sense of order.

A different location is available but no one has had time to get it organized. In return for the help the men have given them, Harding and Dobias use their spare time to organize the new space and set up a general supply control system.

Everybody not on duty is outside to watch GMB as she leaves. Col. Hartz is at the controls and he circles the field with a special dip of the wings to salute the men who are already starting the job of placing field markings. Plattsburg Barracks is the first success for the Mission to establish a chain of landing fields all marked in the same manner.

Next destination: the Curtiss Aeroplane and Motor Company, just outside Buffalo. Distance is about 350 miles and flying time should be just under five hours.

It will be interesting to see the Curtiss plant. It's where the best known of all the American-built aeroplanes is built. Officially it's labeled JN-4 but it's better known as "Jenny".

The air at 6,400 feet is smooth and pleasantly cool and the Libertys maintain a steady beat as GMB moves westward. Harmon nudges Col. Hartz and points toward the gasoline gauges just beyond the windshield. Both gauges indicate empty. He shakes his head. Can't be. They've only been in the air four hours. But the Curtiss factory is not in sight and they can't afford to take a chance.

They set down in a field near a town appropriately called Gasport. Harding and Dobias remove the gauges, swish them in a jar of alcohol, shake them dry and reinstall them. They are working again, showing gas in the tanks. By four o'clock GMB is back in the air.

The Curtiss Plant, four miles north of Buffalo is easily identified. On the property are two large hangars, a small office building and a long landing area marked by red flags.

Lt. Smith enters a warning in the log: Pilots should be careful to keep in the center of the paved area so as to avoid 3-foot flags that mark the edges of the landing surface.

Curtiss mechanics help with servicing the motors and on Saturday morning, as an expression of appreciation for their hospitality, company executives are invited to go for a sight-seeing trip over Niagara Falls.   On the way back, oil pressure drops and by the time the problem is found and corrected it's 4:30.

At 5:00 o'clock. GMB is off and climbing to 4,500 feet for the 188-mile run to the Martin factory in Cleveland.

There are no weather forecasts available but Lt. Harmon recognizes distant cloud shapes that indicate violent storms between them and their destination.   He's had enough of thunderstorms. Better to sit this one out on the ground.

Good luck is flying with them.   Directly ahead is the small town of Willoughby, Ohio. It has a good air port operated by the Cleveland Aero Club, with service for land and sea planes. It's a safe place to sit out the violent electrical storm that sweeps through.

On the morning of the 31st the air is crystal clear but headwinds are strong at 3,000 feet. Flying time for the 12 miles to the Martin plant: 25 minutes.

It is Sunday and the Martin plant is shut down, but the two volunteers who had helped re-build GMB in Farmer Howard's field, have come in to welcome GMB home. They take the crew on a tour through the building, pointing out the efficiency of the production line devised by factory supervisor Larry Bell.

"Mr. Martin insists on the best materials," they say with great pride as they lead the crew through a storeroom.   "And Mr. Douglas, our chief engineer, he knows how to put them together.   So the machines we're building now will be even better than the one you're flying."

First thing Monday morning GMB is moved into a corner of the big building and given a meticulous going over. Harding, Dobias and Harmon follow along, asking questions, learning new techniques, adding to their store of knowledge. By late afternoon a new coat of varnish is on fuselage and wings and Tuesday morning is spent reorganizing and re-packing the cargo compartment.

Col. Hartz shows up with a reporter from the *Cleveland Plain Dealer* and factory test pilot Eric Springer goes along to take the reporter on an aerial tour of the City.

By Tuesday afternoon, with work on GMB completed and all publicity flights done, the crew gets together to plan the next leg of the trip. Using automobile road maps for Ohio, Michigan and Illinois, the distance to Detroit and on to Chicago, adds up to slightly less than 450 miles.

"We should get to Chicago on the afternoon of the fourth," Lt. Smith says.

CHAPTER VII

PROBLEMS HIGH AND LOW

September 3, 4, and 5

Wednesday morning while GMB is being fueled, the Col. and Lt. Smith talk with Glenn Martin and Donald Douglas about uses of aeroplanes for military operations and the benefits air transportation will bring to civilian communities.

Martin expresses his belief that "Too much stress cannot be put upon the importance of every city having in close proximity to its center, an aerial landing field."

He also agrees on the importance of uniformity of field design and marking and promises to apply Air Service markings to the factory air field.

By 1:30 Wednesday afternoon GMB and the crew are ready to go and they head north toward Detroit. Lt. Smith's ankle is giving him trouble and Col. Hartz suggests that they change places. Until the ankle is healed, Lt. Smith will act as terrain observer. He describes the country beneath them as having good landing spots, except for ten miles of swampy land along the shores of Lake Erie near Toledo.

The City of Detroit and the 12 hangars at Morrow Field are in sight when the temperature on the port motor begins to rise. Harmon elects to land there rather than gamble on reaching the Air Service base at Selfridge Field. He backs off power, puts GMB into a shallow glide, and does another of his perfect three-point landings.

Harding and Dobias skip the post-flight routines and instead search for the cause of the temperature rise. The answer quickly becomes obvious: a bird strike has damaged the radiator.

Col. Hartz looks at the damage and tells them, "Don't waste time on repairs. Over at Selfridge Field they've been doing some testing on the Liberty 400s so they should have a spare radiator. I'll call and ask them to fly one over."

The replacement is delivered within the hour but It's dark by the time it's installed and tested. They must stay over night.

Early on the morning of the 5th they depart Detroit and follow the Michigan Central double track rail line half way across the state to Camp Custer.

It has a good field with an excellent approach. GMB and her crew again are welcome excitement for personnel. The Commanding Officer pays close attention as Col. Hartz explains Air Service specifications for identical markings on all landing fields and promises that the marking will be done as soon as materials can be obtained.

The stay at Camp Custer is short and at 1:26 GMB climbs to 5,400 feet. It's only 143 miles to Chicago but a strong headwind reduces ground speed to 60 miles an hour. Keeping the Lake Michigan shoreline in sight Col. Hartz checks the automobile road maps and identifies towns named Decatur, Dowagiac and Buchannon.

Further along he identifies Fort Wayne, Indiana and the name of the town brings to mind a report saying the City plans to purchase a 70 acre tract of land to build an aviation field. He writes himself a reminder to send them a set of designs and field marking specs.

At 19 minutes after three they touch down on the 3,300-foot landing area in Washington Park. All five men are looking forward to a few hours of sight-seeing around one of the country's most exciting cities.

The Liberty motors have cooled down and been shut off when the Chicago police show up and ask them to go somewhere else.

Washington Park is a public recreation area with many baseball diamonds and during the weekend the park will be crowded. The police cannot guarantee the safety of the machine.

" This is a rotten time for us," the Officer in Charge explains. We've had our hands full with strikes and race riots all summer and now we're hearing rumors of more violence planned during the next couple weeks. We can't spare the manpower to guard your machine. You guys are Army Air Service and this landing area is used by the Air Mail so we can't order you to move, but we'd sure appreciate it if you could take the aeroplane to another field."

A man standing nearby steps forward. "I'm a member of the Chicago Aero club and we'd be proud to have you use our field. We have hangars and all the services you need. The field is a mile and a half southwest of the City. Easy to spot from the air."

Col. Hartz responds. "Thank you. We appreciate your hospitality":

September 6

First thing Saturday morning there are three publicity flights. Reporters from the local papers and executives of the Chicago Aero Club enjoy the privilege of a ride in the Army's newest

- 57 -

bomber. It's good public relations and the reporters promise stories to rouse public opinion and let the powers-that-be in Washington hear how strongly the Chicago press and people feel about the importance of increased appropriations for military aeronuatical development.

In addition, the Aero Club people promise to mark their field according to Air Service specs. The Mission to create an airway route of identically marked ground facilities is moving ahead nicely.

With a feeling of accomplishment, the crew and GMB leave Chicago for the 85 miles flight to Milwaukee. Flying time is only 58 minutes.

Milwaukee County Air Port is under construction and one concrete landing area has already been completed. But for reasons never learned, all four tires collapse as GMB touches down.

CHAPTER VIII

DELAYED AGAIN

September 7 through 13

With the help of well-trained air port workers, GMB is moved to a mooring area where there are iron rings set in cement and an automobile is provided to take the crew into town. The first order of business is a wire to McCook Field ordering four new tires. McCook acknowledges, promising tires will be shipped immediately which means they should arrive within four days.

While they wait, the City of Milwaukee extends its hospitality. Colonel Hartz meets with local officials. They welcome his counsel and advice about the air port they are building.

Lt. Harmon hosts a steady stream of visitors who bring food and beverages and a genuine interest in the aeroplane. News of their crash has been in the Milwaukee papers but Lt. Harmon downplays the trauma and the efforts to rebuild the machine. Harding and Dobias help answer questions when they're not busy tightening nuts and bolts, adjusting wires, and doing other small maintenance chores.

Lt. Smith requests a transfer back to Air Service Headquarters. His injured ankle is still very sore and needs special treatment. His request is granted and he takes the first train out of Milwaukee.

That evening Col. Hartz informs the crew of Lt. Smith's departure. "You'll have an inexperienced second pilot for the rest of the trip."

Harmon grins. "That's fine with me. Flying this bird is easier than flying some of the fighters and you've flown her enough to know you just have to stay on the controls. She has a tendency to wallow, especially when the wind is coming in from the side. Some adjustments to the tail assembly would probably fix it but that's a job for the factory."

Harding agrees. "Last time we checked we found one control cable that needed adjusting and that may help some but we can't do enough to eliminate the problem."

"Now that's a surprise," Col. Hartz says with a smile . "After what we've been through, I thought you two could fix anything."

"We're willing to try," Dobias answers, "But like Lt. Harmon says, the problem is in the design of the vertical fins. They need to be bigger or set at different angles."

Col. Hartz makes a note to include a recommendation for rudder changes in his final report. It is an appropriate part of their Mission to test the air frame.

The new tires that were supposed to be shipped out of Dayton immediately, do not arrive for eight days. But the eight days are very well spent. Efforts to inform the public and make friends for the Air Service, pay off handsomely. To the good people of Milwaukee all the crew are heroes and what they have to say about the future of travel by air is given careful attention.

Col. Hartz works with the County Officials to complete detailed plans for their Air Port. They accept his ideas and recommendations and express approval of the proposal for standard designs and markings.

Every day brings an invitation to speak at a luncheon or a dinner being put on by social and business groups and the Colonel makes the most of every opportunity to emphasize the importance of air services for military defense of the country and as a way to tie civilian communities together.

Despite all the hospitality the wait for the tires is annoying. Winter weather can come early in this part of the country and as GMB follows her route west, the chances of bad weather will increase. On Friday evening the crew gets together to plan the next leg of the flight. Assuming that the tires will arrive on Saturday as promised, they set their departure date for Sunday, the 14th.

Col. Hartz recalls a rumor that the mail service intends to make La Cross a regular stop on the route between Chicago and Minneapolis. "It's a good stop for us," he tells the crew. "We can examine the landing strip they already have and talk with City Officials to see if they've heard anything definite about the Army extending its mail service route this far west."

They decide to stay over night at La Crosse, depart early on the morning of the 15th for St. Paul/Minneapolis, stay over night, and head west toward Fargo, North Dakota on the 17th.

Lt. Harmon pulls out the automobile road map for Minnesota.

" Northwest out of Saint Paul we can follow the Mississippi River to St. Cloud. The country beyond that all the way to Fargo is dotted with lakes but most of the way we can keep the railroad tracks in sight."

Harding speaks up. "A private flyer I was talking to yesterday told me this time of year the weather is usually pretty good. He said It's kind of a lull between summer and winter storms."

The Colonel nods. "Weather will be an important factor from here on." He pauses a moment, then continues, "I wonder if the railroads would be willing to help. They have to keep a close eye on weather and they have telegraph connections between stations so they can pass along information. They know the lay of the land too, and can point out clear areas where we could set down near their tracks in case of emergency. Tomorrow when I make my speech to the Milwaukee Chamber of Commerce, at least one of the railroads will probably be represented. I'll try to set up a meeting."

The meeting is successful.

Officials from the Great Northern and the Chicago, St. Paul and Puget Sound railroads are pleased to be asked to help. They will provide weather information and route maps showing their rights-of-way and cleared sections along their tracks. And they'll also provide a list of stations and the names of their station agents.

One of the railroad men makes a suggestion. "Use our telegraph system to keep our station agents advised of your progress. Before you leave one city, let our agent know where you're headed and what time you expect to get there. He'll telegraph the city you're going to and if you don't show up within a reasonable amount of time, we'll tell our engineers and conductors to look for you."

It's the beginning of cooperation between railroad men and fliers that will effect the future of both kinds of transportation.

September 13

The tires arrive from McCook Field and Harding and Dobois get them mounted, Lt. Harmon gives a newspaper reporter a ride over the city and a truck delivers high test gasoline to fill the tanks.

Dobias counts the remaining cans of aviation oil as he pulls out what he needs to service the motors and tells Harding, "We're getting low on oil. We better order it now and have it shipped to Fargo." Harding agrees and the order goes out that night.

With new tires on her wheels, GMB is ready to go again. Col. Hartz will now ride in the control pit full time.

A crowd gathers to see them off, cheering and waving as GMB climbs to 4,500 feet for the 175 mile flight to La Cross. They pass Spring Green at 11:42 and Col. Hartz writes in the log "excellent fields all through Wisconsin River Valley. Landings can be made anyplace."

CHAPTER IX

COOPERATION CONFIRMED

September 14 through 17

Half an hour out of Milwaukee the terrain below changes: ".hills everywhere and timber. No possible landings" but when they reach La Crosse it's a pleasant surprise to find an excellent field under preparation by the city.

Townspeople pour out to see GMB. It is the first big aeroplane to land at their air field. Town fathers tell the Colonel that a local citizen donated the property. They aren't too sure of exactly how the field should be laid out, and the Colonel's offer to help is gladly accepted. While he works with local builders and helps put plans on paper for future reference, Lt. Harmon flies two sight-seeing trips for reporters and photographers. The possibility of air mail service is not mentioned.

September 15 and 16

Next stop, St. Paul. Distance: 132 miles. The Colonel takes GMB to 6,500 feet, and is pleased that the railroad weather forecasts of clear skies are accurate.

Lt. Harmon makes the log entries. 'Landings can be made anywhere in this section of Wisconsin and Minnesota, but with care as fields are on the tops of hills and are rolling'.

It is early afternoon when they set down at the air field in St. Paul.

The rest of the afternoon and all day Friday are filled with doing routine maintenance and publicity flights. The Colonel meets with local people, does a speech for the Rotary Club and talks with top executives in the home office of the Great Northern Railroad.

He explains the suggestion made by the man in Milwaukee about keeping in touch with the railroad from station to station. The top executives like the idea and promise cooperation. "By all means do it. We'll tell our people to give you all the help they can."

That's the good news. The bad news, according to Great Northern's Minneapolis Trackmaster, is nasty weather west of Fargo.

September 17

GMB leaves St. Paul at 11:22 AM and makes a quick stop at the town of Montevideo, Minnesota. It's a political gesture. One of the more influential Congressmen is from here and he has indicated to Air Service Headquarters that a stop would be appreciated.

Montervideo is a pleasant small town and the couple hours on the ground are well spent. But in the back of Harmon's mind is the railroad forecast of bad weather ahead.

In late afternoon GMB heads for Fargo along a course roughly parallel to the Minnesota River. At 4,000 feet it's a pleasant ride and a wind at their back cuts flying time to just an hour and ten minutes. The last ten minutes again prove the dependability of railroad weather information. Freezing rain is falling in Fargo.

Col. Hartz wires a report to Air Service Headquarters: " Arrived Fargo this evening. Weather permitting will proceed to Bismark on 18th after addressing local Chamber of Commerce. 19th to Glendive and Miles City, Montana. 20th to Billings and Helena."

Chapter X

HIGH AND MIGHTY FINE FLYING

September 18 through 22

The rains continue, turning Fargo's three-quarter-mile-square landing field into what Lt. Harmon describes as gumbo mud. Despite the mud, he manages to do one publicity flight. Heavy weather between Fargo and Bismark keep them on the ground and Col. Hartz uses the time to meet with local officials and encourage them to develop the landing field into a full fledged air port.

He tells the group, "When the rains stop and the ground dries out so you can roll it and compact it, you will have the base for an excellent air port."

They are pleased with the praise and describe what they hope to accomplish when construction work is resumed in the spring of 1920. Col. Hartz explains the Air Service marking plan and though no promises are made, he gets the impression that it will be used.

Weather west of Fargo is reported as "clearing", but the station agent for Great Northern Railroad recommends they wait until the next morning to take off for Bismark. All four men make the most of the additional time to show off GMB and again talk about the importance of aeroplanes and air transportation for military and civilian uses.

Harmon, Harding and Dobias have developed a routine for showing the inside of the fuselage and explaining how seats for passengers can be installed. Claims about the future of flying machines are met with good natured skepticism and there ar repeats of the common phrase "if God meant men to fly, He woul have given him wings".

A Sunday school teacher standing nearby points to GMB and say quietly, "I think He has."

Col. Hartz meantime, is involved in discussions about the need fo good roads leading to the air port. "Moving construction equipmen and supplies to the site will be easier if a solid road is built firs And when the air port is open for business, a good road systen will make the difference between success and failure."

Harding and Dobias check for the supply of aviation oil they ha asked be shipped to Fargo but find only half of what they ordered They ask the Colonel to order another shipment sent to Missoula Montana.

Despite the supply difficulties, the stop over in Fargo is a pleasan experience for everyone and next morning when GMB is preparing to leave for Bismark, most of the townspeople are at the field to wave good-by.

At 11:50 GMB lifts off, heading west. It's slightly less than 20C miles to Bismark . The rain has moved out but there are scattered clouds and Harmon climbs above them to 6,500 feet. The air is smooth despite steady headwinds that hold ground speed down to 60 miles an hour.

Col. Hartz observes terrain and adds to the log: "Landings can be made practically any place, but pilots must be very cautious as country is deceptive, owing to color and many sharp ditches and arroyas."

At Bismark there is a nicely prepared landing field on a piece of land owned by the federal government. The City regards the location as an ideal spot for an air port that will serve both military and civilian needs and with cooperation of the local military commander, has cleared the land and marked off the smoothest portion for a landing area.

City officials tell Col. Hartz they are willing to continue the improvements and are also willing to maintain the landing field. But in return the City wants a long term lease on the land and guarantees of unlimited access to the field.

Hartz likes the idea and promises to send it along to Headquarters. He sends it first to General Mitchell, knowing he is always open to new ideas and will pass this one along to General Menoher who will, in turn, pass it along through channels to whatever government department has jurisdiction over that particular piece of land.

The crew manages a good night's sleep and early in the morning Lt. Harmon takes a newspaper reporter for a ride.

At one o'clock on the afternoon of the 20th GMB departs Bismark for the small town of Glendive which is home to one of Montana's elected representatives in Washington. It's another political stop and the Congressman has told his constituents to expect the visit. GMB is the first aeroplane to land anywhere near Glendive and the whole town turns out.

There are welcoming speeches followed by a hearty meal and discussions about the benefits aeroplanes can bring to the town. Colonel Hartz is asked to select a site for a permanent landing field when the town has the money to build it. He selects the field where GMB landed, sketches a design, and shares his knowledge with the men who will be in charge of construction.

Glendive hospitality is typically western and it's 11:55 the next morning before GMB circles the town to say good-by and turns to follow the Yellowstone River south to Miles City. Fields on both sides of the river offer enough space for an emergency landing.

Miles City puts on its best small town welcome and Lt. Harmon flies two flights to give a reporter and several city officials a thrill and their first view of their home town from the air.

September 22

Col. Hartz checks with the railroad Stationmaster for latest weather, tells him of the next leg of their trip, and wires Headquarters.

"Will proceed to Billings tonight, then to Helena on the 23rd weather permitting. It is very cold with snow flurries. From Helena to Missoula on the 23rd, stop briefly, then continue on to Coeur d'Alene, Idaho. The 24th to Spokane, Washington and to Seattle on the 25th"

He is leaving the telegraph office as a wire is coming in. "It's for you," the telegrapher says, "from the Mayor of Glendive."

The wire reads: "Thought you might be pleased to know that work on our landing field has just started."

Col. Hartz says thank you and as he walks out of the telegraph office he mentally adds the name of Glendive, Montana to the four other communities that have promised to build air ports or landing fields.   He is satisfied with the way their mission to promote construction of air ports and landing fields is working.

By 11 o'clock GMB is serviced, the motors are warmed up and they're ready to head out for Billings. Although there are no high mountains along the route, Lt. Harmon chooses to climb to 8,700 feet. The air is cold and everybody's glad they're wearing fleece lined suits and boots.

The Yellowstone River and the railroad tracks are good guides. Col. Hartz notes in the log that there are good fields that could be used for emergency landings along both sides of the River. Flying time to Billings is one hour and 56 minutes.

As has become routine, there are meetings with officials, speeches to civic groups, and publicity flights. Again the Colonel is asked to select a site for a landing field. He likes the field where GMB landed and recommends they start by constructing a concrete road leading to the site. He answers questions about field grading and installation of lights. Later that evening he prepares a formal report for Headquarters beginning "The people of the West have been very enthusiastic in regard to fields ..."

Weather is good but temperatures are dropping. They will stay overnight in Miles City. It's another delay but starting the motors under very cold weather conditions is an involved procedure of draining oil and water, then heating both fluids before they are poured back. Getting the warmed fluids pulled through the motors prior to starting is essential and not something to be done in a hurry.

CHAPTER XI

FIRE AND ICE

September 23 through 27

It is mid-morning as GMB circles Billings. The men are thoroughly chilled. It's been a very cold two hours, at 8,700 feet. For a landing site Lt. Harmon selects an open field some four miles west of town.

Townspeople have heard the aeroplane and the crew barely has GMB securely moored when the first horsemen and the first truckload of visitors arrive.

Col. Hartz greets each person and introduces the crew. Lt. Harmon talks about their trip and Dobias and Harding take turns explaining the aeroplane. It's a happy morning and when one of the town leaders asks the Colonel how they should go about deciding on a place to build a landing field, he and Lt. Harmon fire up the Liberty motors and take four of the city's leading citizens for a ride over the area.

From the vantage point in the nose pit, Col. Hartz points to the field where GMB landed and another one nearby, saying both are low lying and are apt to be a problem during wet weather. The site he thinks is best is on high ground about a mile west of town.

The official riding beside him responds, "That's called Table Rock and it's close to 640 acres. Owned by one of our prominent families and I'm not sure they would sell."

Col. Hartz nods, then says, "Can we ask them?"

When they get back to the field a newspaper reporter is waiting and Lt. Harmon takes him on a circuit of the area. It looks as if all the residents of Billings have congregated at the landing field. They wait patiently for Lt. Harmon to return, and with GMB firmly moored, the crew accepts frontier hospitality that provides a ride into town and food, food and more food.

After dinner there is a constant stream of visitors and Col. Hartz is pleased when he learns that the owners of the land he selected as the landing field site, will donate it to the City if the Colonel is willing to prepare the design. He quickly sketches a layout and goes over the diagram with the town fathers. They are happy to have the benefits of his expert guidance and promise that grading, paving the road leading to the site, and installation of a lighting system will begin immediately.

It is late afternoon before the crew can get away from the enthusiasm of the good citizens of Billings and for the next two hours, flying at 8,200 feet on a heading for Helena, Hartz is content to observe terrain but sees no flat spaces that appear to be large enough for an emergency landing.

Twenty-two minutes later they cross over the town of Townsend, and once again there are good fields below .

It is nearly dusk as Harmon guides GMB around the Capitol Building in Helena, then continues on to land at what appears to be a smooth and level part of the Fort Harrison Military Reservation. He doesn't see the weathered wood rail fence that zigzags across the middle of the area when he puts GMB on the ground. The landing is perfect. Tall grass grabs the tail skid, slowing forward momentum. GMB stops with her nose over the fence.

Once again the sound of the aeroplane has brought out city officials and there is much discussion about the possible need for an air field. GMB and the crew decide to stay at the Fort and discussions about how to set up the landing field continue into the late evening. It is a City official who suggests the same kind of set-up that had been proposed by the City of Bismark, North Dakota, but with a slightly different twist.

Helena officials want it clearly understood that the field will be open to all aeroplanes, regardless of ownership, and there must be unrestricted access for automobiles and other ground vehicles, to the part of Fort Harrison where the air port will be located. If these two points are approved and if the two governments can negotiate a mutually agreeable land lease, the City of Helena will underwrite the cost of removing obstacles such as the zigzag fence, grading the site, and building areoplane service facilities. Then when the field is open for use, they will be maintain control over the facility, operating it as another city-owned public utility.

The Colonel wires the offer to Headquarters.

Wednesday is a crisp and clear as the crew gets GMB ready for the flight to Missoula.

A check with the railroad station agent warns of nasty weather building along the route. An early winter storm has dumped snow on the higher elevations and is headed east.

"We'll need our warmest winter gear, " Hartz tells the crew. What they don't have they requisition from Fort Harrison supplies. The sheepskin-lined boots, flying suits and special helmets are heavy but the warmth is welcome.

The distance to Missoula is 90 miles and 80 miles of it is misery. In addition to the early fall icy blizzard conditions, smoke from still smoldering forest fires cuts down visibility.

Col. Hartz observes that "landings could be made in many places in this valley" and "the large field on the Fort Missoula Reservation would be excellent if dragged." They set down in a 2,000-foot square field next to the fair grounds. It's one of the best prepared landing areas they have encountered.

When Harding and Dobias ask for the supplies that were supposed to have been shipped in, they get blank stares and mumbles of "what supplies?" There's no aviation oil and for the first time in their travels, obtaining gasoline is a serious problem.

The local automobile gasoline distributor has high test gasoline but will only provide enough to fill GMB's tanks. He flatly refuses to deplete his supply by selling them spare drums of gas and he says he never heard of anything called aviation oil.

The colonel wires Headquarters: "Great difficulty is being encountered in this section owing to lack of supply of satisfactory gasoline and oil. The District offices of the oil companies object to shipping their drums beyond their district lines. The Express Company will not handle high test gasoline and it is hard for Commercial Clubs or Chambers of Commerce to procure it."

The crew knows that with full tanks and decent weather there is adequate fuel to get to Spokane, but if there is an emergency of any kind, the lack of reserves could be the difference between life and death.

Even more important is the oil. Without adequate lubrication the motors will seize up and that will put them down long before the gasoline runs out. Once again Harding and Dobias put their knowledge and ingenuity to work.

They've been around aeroplanes and motors long enough to remember the days before aviation oil was created from petroleum and oil pressed from castor beans was the common lubricant. It stinks when it burns and it spews a fine yellow residue that's difficult to remove from whatever surface it attaches to, but if it's available, it will be an acceptable substitute.

Asking around town, they finally locate a source and persuade the Missoula Drug Company to sell them 30 gallons of castor oil. It should be enough to keep the motors running smoothly until they can replenish their supply of aviation oil.

Weather in the Missoula area is clearing but the railroad people warn that another storm is brewing to the west, between Missoula and GMB's next destination .. Spokane, Washington.

Forest fires in the area have recreated themselves despite the snow, but no one is sure of their exact location or how much territory they cover. Colonel Hartz knows that Army aeroplanes have been used to scout fire areas in California and he sees this as an opportunity to demonstrate how the use of aeroplanes can be important to the civilian community. The lumbering industry is a major economic factor in this part of the country.

He offers the use of GMB to follow the smoke to the burning areas so the Forest Service people can see exactly where the fires are and the direction in which they are traveling. The offer is accepted and they make two 100-mile trips to the town of Dixon and back to Missoula.

It is an effective demonstration of how useful an aeroplane can be and is a persuasive argument in favor of building an air port. When the Colonel explains what the City of Helena proposes to do if the federal government will sign a long term land lease, Missoula officials say they are willing to try for the same arrangement at Fort Missoula. If that doesn't work, there is still the site near near the Fairgrounds. At one place or the other, the City will build an air port with service facilities, including gasoline.

"Too bad the air port's not in place today," Col. Hartz says.

The lack of adequate fuel continues to be a frustration but it's bad weather that keeps them grounded for two more days. Finally, on Sunday, the skies begin to clear.

Before they leave for Spokane, Col. Hartz advises Washington "Gasoline arrived here today from Lewiston, Idaho, on a special order from me. This, together with rain, has caused a three day delay, but even if the weather had been good I would have been forced to remain here, owning to lack of gasoline.

"I recommend that if future flights are contemplated, arrangement be made with each Chamber of Commerce to keep a permanent supply of high test gasoline and standard oils on hand at all times for use of Government planes only. This could be purchased by the Supply Board and stored at certain central points along the line of flight."

CHAPTER XII

TIME TO SPARE, GO BY AIR

September 28 through October 3

It's an ill wind that blows no good, and thanks to the blizzard, the forest fires are finally out and the skies are clear of the smokey overcast.

While Col. Hartz is firing off another wire to Washington, the crew is doing cold weather pre-flight routines.

Water for the radiators is heated and poured into the tanks and the castor oil is also warmed. Turning the propellers with all ignition switches off, distributes the hot liquids through the motors. Harding and Dobias signal Harmon, he calls out "switches on." One pull of the propellers and the big Libertys fire up. Harmon changes throttle settings to test that they are functioning properly, then throttles back to idle.

Meantime the crowd of spectators grows steadily larger as townspeople, soldiers from Fort Missoula and every forest ranger in the area come out to watch the departure.

At 3:15 on Sunday afternoon, waves and shouts of "good-by and God speed" follow GMB as she lifts off and turns west to follow the tracks of the Great Northern Railroad. Harmon calls them his iron compass and will keep them in sight as proof they are on course during the 220-mile flight to Spokane.

Earlier this morning the Stationmaster at Missoula had said the weather conditions were not good, but would improve as the day progressed.

Rain that had been pouring on Spokane for several days ha reduced to drizzle as GMB sets down on the flying field. It is larg enough but Col. Hartz describes it in the log as "otherwise ver poor having but one landing area and grounds to the sides ar rocky. On one side of the field there is a sheer drop into the river 1 or 20 feet blow. On the other side is a wide road sufficiently ditche to upset a plane."

During a meeting with the city fathers, he recommends a larg section of land south of where they landed, saying "this would mak an excellent field. "

His report to Headquarters describes the status of the landing field "At present the City has leased the field under a three-year contac to the Northwestern Aero Club. This does not restrict ship alighting or leaving but does restrict free use, and rent is charged For this reason the field would be unsatisfactory for permanen government use such as mail service, etc."

September 29, 30, October 1, 2, and 3

It is a sunny morning as Harmon does a publicity flight for th benefit of the local newspaper. The crew then flies a quick trip t Coeur d'Alene, Idaho and back before the rains return and weathe stops all flying around Spokane. For the next three days weathe keeps them on the ground.

The men make the most of every opportunity to promote thei missions, emphasizing the importance of bigger appropriations fo the Army Air Service, the future of air travel and the importance c all-weather landing fields with service facilities for aeroplanes of a kinds.

Finally, on Friday morning the clouds lift. Harding and Dobias clea mud and dirt from the underside of the fuselage, give the landing gear an especially careful check, make sure all gas tanks are filled, and GMB takes off for Seattle.

The railroad Stationmaster in Spokane had said there would be heavy fog around Seattle and he's right. Seattle is socked in solid.

GMB turns south toward Tacoma and the Camp Lewis Military Reservation. Ground fog is beginning to form and darkness is rapidly approaching as they sight the landing field at Tacoma. Camp Lewis isn't far ahead, but the chances for locating it in the dark are too slim to risk. They land and stay over night in Tacoma.

CHAPTER XIII

CALIFORNIA HERE WE COME

October 4, 5, 6, 7, 8 and 9

Early morning ground fog is thick but lifting as Harding and Dobias go through the regular pre-flight check lists. By mid-morning the fog has burned off and the six mile hop from Tacoma to Camp Lewis is done in 11 minutes.

The troops at Camp Lewis welcome GMB, show the crew where to bunk and provide lunch. There are good working facilities for taking care of the aeroplane and Harmon, Harding and Dobias go into their well-practiced routines for showing off the machine and directing volunteers who offer any help that's needed.

Col. Hartz requests an automobile to drive to Seattle where he has a Saturday night speaking engagement at the Aviation Club. He plans to spend the weekend meeting with influential citizens, using the opportunity to promote the idea of building an air port to serve land based planes. He recognizes the value of the existing base for sea planes but emphasizes the importance of a second facility to serve land planes.

He points out that such an air port would be the western terminus for the air route across the northern tier of states and as such it would be an important stop for long distance flyers. The Air Service is also planning an air route to Alaska and a good landing field in Seattle could become an essential supply station for northbound aeroplanes.

Meanwhile Harmon and Harding and Dobias are being treated as honored guests by the troops at Camp Lewis.

October 5

Everybody attends worship services and during the calm and quiet of Sunday afternoon the GMB crew and air men stationed at Camp Lewis, get together to talk about – what else? – aeroplanes and flying. For the benefit of the Camp Lewis people, Harmon explains the purpose of their flight.

"We have four main Missions .. to test the Liberty Motors, test the strength of the fuselage, lay out a pattern of airports roughly 200 miles apart along the borders of the country, and convince people that aeroplanes are the future of transportation."

There are questions about GMB's performance and maintenance problems with the motors. The afternoon passes quickly as the three crew members recount their experiences and leave the impression that this big bomber, designed and built by Americans, is better than any other flying machine produced anywhere in the world.

Setting up a system of air ports and landing fields is progressing nicely. Harding tells the group, "Col. Hartz has met with officials in every city we've visited. He's very convincing when he talks about how important aeroplanes are going to be and how smaller cities will benefit if they have an air port with ground services."

Dobias adds his own praise of the Colonel. "He's also very concerned about our safety and one of the best things he's done is the arrangement we have with the railroads. They provide us with weather reports and maps of their tracks. We let stationmasters know when we're leaving one town and what time we expect to get to the next one. When we land we tell the local stationmaster and he wires back to the town we left.

The safety angle is that if we don't report when we land at the next town, the stationmaster there will send a wire to the stationmaster at the town we left to let him know we didn't arrive. And both of them will alert crews on the next trains coming along, to look for us. It's good to know that if we have a forced landing, somebody is keeping track of us and has an idea of where we might be. There's an awful lot of uninhabited country out here in the west."

Harding and Dobias talk about the crack-up, explaining what they did to rebuild the aeroplane. They also point out that there have been only two emergency landings due to mechanical failures and both problems were easily repaired. When someone suggests that what they're doing requires a lot of courage, they shrug.

What's courage? This is an assignment. The Army has given us the training and the tools we need to do the job. There are times when it's not fun and there have been times when we would rather have been anywhere else but in that aeroplane with freezing rain pouring down on us. But it's all part of flying.

Harding adds, "We learn something new practically every day. Weather is still one of our biggest problems but we've learned that certain types of clouds can give us clues to what's ahead. We've learned how to judge a field under us and decide whether it's a place to land in an emergency. And we've learned how much we can accomplish with common tools and common sense."

Lt. Harmon interrupts. "These two guys have given a new meaning to the word ingenuity. They've done the impossible more than once. I've already recommended to Col. Hartz that Army Air Service Pilots should be taught how to do basic repairs (groans from the flyers) .and maybe it would be a good idea if mechanics get a couple hours of flying time". (Cheers from the mechanics.)

Harmon laughs and continues, "I've learned a lot on this trip and I'll always be glad I've had the opportunity. I'll never earn a rating as an engineer or be a full-fledged mechanic, but thanks to the Sergeants, I can do simple repairs and sometimes when you have an emergency landing, a simple repair will get the machine back in the air."

Late in the afternoon newspaper reporters and photographers show up. Lt. Harmon does two separate sight-seeing tours for them, then takes Camp Lewis officers for a ride around the area. It's dusk when the last flight lands.

Col. Hartz is back from Seattle. After supper the crew makes plans for the next leg of the flight. They have maps for Oregon and California and Col. Hartz points to the cities where they will land: Portland and Medford in Oregon and Sacramento and San Francisco in California. He wires the Presidio in San Francisco to expect GMB on Friday.

October 6

A whole gang of volunteers help get GMB ready to leave. Harding and Dobias assign cheerful helpers to the miserable job of cleaning the belly. They take buckets of soapy water, clean cloths, and slide under the fuselage to remove all traces of mud. Others help maneuver the heavy drums of gasoline into position and use chamois to filter the fuel as it goes into the tanks.

Purified water is available for the radiators and aviation oil is on hand.

"No more stinking castor oil," Dobias says and Harding nods. "We're taking on a good supply of aviation oil but with a little luck there shouldn't be any supply problems from here on."

Both men cross their fingers. Luck is something they treat with respect.

Camp Lewis to Portland is 154 miles. Hartz climbs GMB up to 7,000 feet and an hour and 42 minutes later they land, in heavy rain, at an excellent field east of the Columbia River and a mile and a half south of the City. Harmon makes a note in the log: "care should be taken to avoid power wires." They secure GMB and hurry inside the nearby barracks.

Dobias settles into a chair at a table, drying off and getting ready to re-fold the automobile maps they've been using. "Hey," he says as he lays maps of Washington and Oregon side by side. "Look at this. We crossed the Columbia River in the middle of Washington, and here we are in Oregon, almost at the Pacific Ocean, and we've crossed the same river again."

Col. Hartz moves over for a look. He traces the river north. "It apparently starts in Canada, flows south across the State of Washington, then turns west across Oregon to the Pacific Ocean. "

Harmon chips in. "1,243 miles long."

Harding says "Show off!" to which Harmon responds, "Just quoting the chamber of commerce."

"And that reminds me, " Col. Hartz says,. "I have a date to speak at the Chamber luncheon tomorrow."

October 7 and 8

Weather remains miserable, keeping GMB on the ground. Col. Hartz wires Washington that they will head south to Medford, Oregon then on to Sacramento, California as soon as weather permits.

October 9

Finally the weather clears enough for the flight to Medford. To get above the last bits of weather and clear the mountains below, Lt. Harmon climbs to 13,000 feet. It takes 2 hours and 20 minutes to cover the 300 miles and their fur-lined clothing is not enough to protect them from the terrible cold. Col. Hartz and Lt. Harmon have trouble working the controls. Their hands and feet are close to being frozen.

With sighs of relief they land in a field beside the main highway, just two miles west of Medford. The landing is no small accomplishment. The field has been planted with alfalfa hay, and it's wet and slippery. Fortunately the plants are tall enough to wrap the tail skid and help bring GMB to a safe stop.

Late in the afternoon GMB heads southeast toward Sacramento. Flying time for the 308 miles is three hours and 15 minutes at 10,000 feet. It's not quite so cold as the previous stretch, but it's still a relief to land at the big government aerodrome east of the City.

CHAPTER XIV

NO SHOW, NO TELL

October 10 through 16

Thursday evening at the government aerodrome in Sacramento is restful. No speeches are scheduled and the only people around are military personnel. With no civilians around to overhear, the conversation is casual and uninhibited as crew members describe how the aeroplane operates and talk about some of the problems they've encountered.

Harmon, Harding and Dobias calmly agree, "It's interesting."

Col. Hartz talks with the men in charge of maintaining the aerodrome operations area, explaining the purpose and style of Air Service markings. With quick and practiced motions, he sketches a lay-out that will serve as guidelines for the work that must be done. Later in the evening the crew meets for their routine route planning session.

Next stop, San Francisco for one night, an over-night stop in Fresno, then on to Los Angeles for two days. After that, south to Rockwell Field at San Diego and a week of rest and relaxation.

"What's Rockwell Field like?" Dobias asks and Harmon describes it as "an island about 7 miles off shore. Began as a Glenn Curtiss aviator training school. Then when the War came along, the Army moved in, expanded the landing area, built barracks and hangars and put in repair and maintenance facilities. It's the biggest and the best of all the Air Service stations in California. And San Diego's a great place to have a good time."

Col. Hartz adds, "We share the island with the Navy and I've heard there are some hard feelings over who's in control."

Harmon laughs. "One of my buddies told me about how the Navy flyers buzz Army planes and the Army buzzes Navy seaplanes. Said it makes flying in and out of Rockwell a lot of fun."

"That kind of fun we don't need," the Colonel says. "We don't want to get involved with local rivalries, so let's watch what we say and do. I want to turn the aeroplane over to the Rockwell maintenance people and let them give it a good going over. "

Harding and Dobias start to object, and the Colonel continues, "Another opinion never hurts and getting an objective assessment of what you two have done to keep us going, will look good on your records. But you are not to let them sandbag you into staying on the Field. Answer basic questions and leave. It's been 78 days since we left Bolling Field and we have no way of knowing how long before we get back. We've faced some tough situations and there may be more ahead. A week of rest and recreation in San Diego was part of the original trip plan and despite all the delays, I see no reason to change the schedule. We'll be back at Bolling when we get there. "

"Thank you, Colonel. We appreciate your concern." Harding says.

Dobias nods. "It'll sure be nice to have nothing to do for a few days."

They stand, stretch, yawn and as they part for their sleeping quarters, each man asks himself the same question: " What next?"

October 10

Early morning is bright and shining when the crew meets for breakfast. Colonel Hartz has already contacted the local railroad people.

"They tell me morning ground fog is normal in San Francisco but it should clear by noon. The only meeting on my schedule is with the Base Commander. The flight shouldn't take more than an hour, so let's plan to leave here at 11. We'll stay over night, and go on to Fresno tomorrow."

At 7,500 feet the air is smooth and cool and the Liberty motors perform with the perfection the crew has come to expect. All things considered, the mission to test the motors has been an outstanding success. According to the manufacturer's specifications, they should have been changed after 50 hours but with close to 70 hours of operating time logged and with what has been basic and minimum maintenance, both motors are functioning far above expectations.

As GMB moves along, Harmon observes the land below and notes in the log book: "excellent fields as far as Fairfield but from there to San Francisco the flight extends over the tide lands and bay and it would be impossible to land."

But it's a beautiful day for flying, the accommodations in San Francisco are first class, and weather forecasts indicate ideal flying conditions. If all goes as planned, three days from now they will be in San Diego with a whole week to rest and relax.

But what's planned is not always what happens.

Col. Hartz had notified the Commandant of the San Francisco Army garrison that GMB would be stopping over, and the Commandant took it upon himself to notify Air Service Headquarters of GMB's arrival time.

October 11, 12, 13 and 14

Morning fog and two publicity flights for newspaper people delay the departure for Fresno until after lunch. By ten o'clock Harding and Dobias have completed pre-flight routines, the fog is slowly burning off, and Harmon starts warming up the motors prior to the publicity flights.

Col. Hartz leaves for a meeting with the Commandant. "I should be back by noon," he says.

It's a surprise when he shows up half an hour later, and still more of a surprise when the crew realize that this man who has remained calm and collected under the worst of circumstances, is boiling mad.

"We're grounded," he growls and extends a telegram. "This just arrived from Headquarters. It tells us we have to wait for the boss himself. Brigadier General Charles T. Menoher is coming out to join us."

In unison Harding and Dobias ask "When?"

Col. Hartz shakes his head. "No dates given. All it says is that we are to wait until he shows up."

So they wait all day Saturday and all day Sunday. On Monday Colonel Hartz sets up meetings with local officials and civic groups.

Before he leaves for a Tuesday luncheon meeting with a group of influential citizens, he wires Headquarters for the third time, asking when the General will arrive. The days of waiting have worn his patience thin.

The exasperation he feels is set aside as he enters the room where lunch is served and the Colonel is his usual affable self as he meets and mingles with the makers and shakers of a great city. One of the persons he meets is the Belgian Counsel.

In a brief speech to the group, Col. Hartz describes GMB and their flight around the country. The Counsel is much impressed. He explains that Belgium's King Albert is touring the United States and one reason for the visit is to examine military equipment, particularly aeroplanes.

"Our Air Service," the Counsel explains, "has fighter planes built by your Glenn Martin. His Highness thinks they are the finest planes we have and I know he would be pleased to examine the plane you are flying."

"We would be honored to have him fly GMB, " Col. Hartz responds. "Would tomorrow be suitable?"

The Counsel shakes his head. "Unfortunately His Highness left for Los Angeles this morning."

"How long will he be there?" the Colonel asks and the Counsel again shakes his head. "I believe he plans to spend a week. He especially wants to meet your movie star, Mr. Douglas Fairbanks."

Colonel Hartz smiles. This is too good an opportunity to miss. If he can arrange a meeting and take King Albert for a ride in GMB it will be a demonstration of international good will that could generate business for the Americans who are trying to build a world wide market for their aeronautical machines.

"Would you contact His Highness and set up a meeting on Saturday the 18th? We have to make an over night stop in Fresno on our way south."

The Counsel is delighted. "Thank you, Colonel. I know His Highness will be most pleased and I think your government should also be pleased."

Col. Hartz isn't sure Headquarters will be pleased. If he takes GMB away from San Francisco before General Menoher arrives, he will be breaking a direct order. He doesn't mind bending the rules, but so obviously breaking them is a serious matter. He decides to wait one more night for the General.

October 15, 16, and 17

On Wednesday morning there is no General and no word from Headquarters about when he might arrive. Col. Hartz walks out and across to the aeroplane where Harmon, Harding and Dobias are doing clean-up chores.

"We leave in 30 minutes," he tells Harmon. "Stop in Fresno over night and go to Los Angeles as early as we can get away on Saturday morning."

He turns and walks quickly back to the office to send a wire notifying Headquarters of their departure for Fresno, advising of . his meeting with the King of Belgium and suggesting that General Menoher could meet them at Chaplin Field in Los Angeles.

He dusts his hands in a 'that's-that' gesture, returns to the aeroplane and GMB takes off for Fresno. It's another of the 200-mile spacings the Air Service regards as the maximum safe distance between landing fields.

From 5,000 feet there is a good view of the country below. Hartz jots down descriptions of what he sees as fairly good fields along the way but adds a note of caution: "care should be taken as this country is thickly cultivated, most of the cultivation being orchard and the rest under irrigation."

Rangers at the Forest Patrol Station two and a half miles from Fresno welcome GMB and help service the aeroplane. It's late afternoon and the men of GMB accept the Rangers' invitation to share their quarters for the night.

Next morning Hartz walks the landing area asking questions to learn what kind of air field the Rangers believe they should have. By evening he has prepared a diagram for creating a facility best suited to their kind of flying. The Rangers like his ideas and agree to mark the area in accordance with Air Service specifications.

If the colonel is worrying about breaking orders from Headquarters by leaving San Francisco, the worry doesn't show.

The distance from Fresno to Los Angeles is roughly 220 miles. At 5,000 feet, in bright California sunshine, flying time is two hours 50 minutes. En route they pass over Visalia .."good field northwest of town .. Bakersfield .. forest patrol station. Tulare .. landings can be made in the vicinity .. extreme care should be taken however, as the country is very sandy."

There is a choice of places to land in Los Angeles and GMB sets down at an excellent field west of the City.

It is a well-equipped private field approximately 2,000 feet from corner to corner, owned by Sidney Chaplin, who operates a flying service catering to the motion picture industry.

Col. Hartz walks over to the field office and arranges to send a telegram to Headquarters reporting their arrival and repeating his plans to meet with the King of Belgium. By the time he returns to the aeroplane a small crowd has assembled to gawk at GMB and talk with her crew.

Standing near the aeroplane is a pleasant looking, well dressed gentleman flanked by two people who walk slightly behind him. He approaches Col. Hartz and asks quietly if it is possible to go for a ride.

Before the Colonel can respond the crowd begins clapping and cheering. They recognize motion picture star Douglas Fairbanks. He too asks if it's possible to go for a ride.

Hartz tells Harmon, "I'll fly them out to Santa Ana and back. Should be about an hour and a half."

Harmon shows Fairbanks how to climb into the nose pit and Hartz assists the other gentleman into the control pit.

When GMB returns to Chaplin Field the unnamed gentleman thanks Hartz , shakes hands with Fairbanks and quietly departs. Photographers ask Fairbanks to pose for pictures and he invites the crew to join him. Hartz is walking across the field toward the office, so it's Harmon and Harding who have their pictures taken with the world famous movie star.

In the office there is a telegram from Headquarters. Col. Hartz reads it, refolds it and takes his time walking back to the aeroplane.

With a straight face he hands the folded paper to Harmon who reads it out loud:

"Do not repeat do not contact King.of Belgium. Your job is to test the aeroplane, not sell it. Proceed to Rockwell Field immediately."

Harmon chuckles as he hands back the telegram. "Does this cancel the order to wait for General Menoher?"

All four crewmen are still laughing as GMB takes off for San Diego.

Douglas Fairbanks   Sgt. Harding   Lt. Harmon

Photo courtesy the American Aviation Historical Society (AAHS)

CHAPTER XV

ROCKWELL, REST AND RECREATION

October 19 through October 28

The San Diego area is a beautiful sight. As GMB glides in for a landing, the waters of the Bay reflect a magnificent sunset . North Island is outlined in gold and Rockwell Field, with its well laid out landing area welcomes the travelers.

In 1910 when the first aeroplane landed on North Island, Glenn Curtiss described it as "a flat, sandy island about four miles long and two miles wide with a number of good fields for landing flights. It is uninhabited except by jackrabbits, cottontails, snipe and quail."

The only buildings were a farm house and an old hay barn which became the first hangar on the Island. Curtiss set up an Aviation Camp and offered the Navy free flight instruction for one officer. Since 1911 both the Army and Navy have used the Island, developing it into a training and maintenance base.

It is one of a very few military installations that has not suffered from the cut backs in funding since the end of the War. Air Service personnel includes 85 officers and 381 enlisted men. There are also 71 civilian employees and to all of them, Rockwell is the best duty station in the country.

On-field facilities include a hospital, photo lab, mess hall, post exchange, aero repair shop, machine shop, warehouses, garage for ground vehicles and hangars for 98 aircraft.

ROCKWELL FIELD

NORTH ISLAND, SAN DIEGO, CALIFORNIA

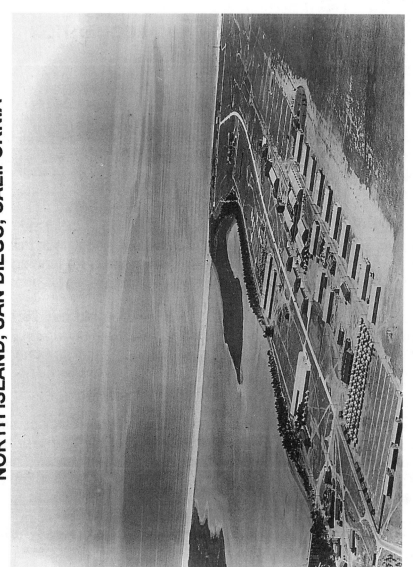

Photograph from the collection of the San Diego Aeronautical Museum

Dobias sums it up. "All this and San Diego too. Aren't we lucky?"

Mechanics and pilots swarm around GMB and like other troops at other bases, glad to have the opportunity to work on the newest machine in the Air Service. Col. Hartz reminds Harmon, Harding and Dobias that they are here for rest and recreation.

Answer whatever questions you get this evening, but tomorrow I want you to relax while you can. I'm going across the Bay to see family and friends and I'll contact the railroad people about getting weather forecasts when we head east at the end of the week."

He also recommends that they all take advantage of the medical facilities and have physical examinations.

Harding and Dobias spend the night in the barracks and the next morning lead the way through an examination of the fuselage, inside and out. By noon they are satisfied that GMB is in good hands and they catch a boat ride across the water to the mainland, ready to make the most of their first real freedom from responsibility since they departed Bolling Field on the 24th of July.

When they return to the Island at the end of the week, they report to the medical facilities for their physicals. Col. Hartz and Lt. Harmon join them. All four men are in excellent condition.

October 28 and 29

GMB is pronounced ready for a test flight. Hartz and Harmon take her to Los Angeles, stay over night, and return to San Diego the next morning. Everything seems to be in good working order.

The crew meets for their regular planning session. Harmon says, "The flight to El Paso will be the longest leg of the trip. I'd like to see if we can make it non-stop."

Col. Hartz smiles and asks, "In a hurry to get home?" and the three men chorus an emphatic "yes."

He nods. "We can try. According to the railroad weather people we should have a strong wind at our back. But if we have to land somewhere along the way, there are improved landing fields all the way across the State of Arizona."

Dobias adds, "And all that desert, too."

"Let's concentrate on staying in the air," Hartz says and Harmon adds, "This is a chance to set a time and distance record for two motor aeroplanes. It would be a good accomplishment to add to the report when we get back to Bolling Field."

CHAPTER XVI

GO EAST, YOUNG MEN

October 30

Today is the beginning of the last leg of the around the rim flight. The route they have planned will take them across Arizona, Texas, Louisiana, around the Florida Peninsula, then north over Georgia, the Carolinas, Virginia and finally, back to Bolling Field.

East from El Paso there are military air ports now vacant, but well known and easily identified. The men are rested, the fuselage, landing gear and motors have been gone over and declared to be in good shape. This should be the easiest part of the trip.

The motors have handled as much as five hours of steady flying. Will they handle eight? If so, it will be a good way to sum up the testing program and complete Mission Number One.

Mission Number Two, which was to evaluate the aeroplane's ability to stand up under less than ideal field conditions with minimum maintenance, is completed. GMB is getting tired and small repairs are a constant demand, but the framework has held up very well. There is no doubt that this is a very well built, very tough, machine.

Mission Number three was to show the aeroplane to the public and explain its potential as transportation serving both military and civilian needs. This has been done in 33 cities where GMB and her crew have landed and as part of that effort, they have flown 47 courtesy and publicity flights. There is no record of how many speeches Col. Hartz has made but he has received verification that air ports are either being planned or are already under construction in 15 of the places where they've stopped.

The only part of Mission Number Four still to do, is terrain observation. It won't be difficult. Training programs for flyers and other Army personnel and military excursions, have fairly well catalogued this part of the country.

Army Air Service training operations are now at an all time low because of cuts in appropriations but several of the established fields are being used by the Border Patrol, by civilian pilots, and anybody else who happens along.

October 30

At 8 o'clock in the morning Rockwell Field is humming with activity. GMB has been serviced, pre-flight inspections are finished, and they're ready to roll on what they hope will be a record-setting 850 mile non-stop ride.

The flyers at Rockwell recommend a climb to 10,000 feet. This will be high enough to get them over the mountains, and if the following winds materialize, GMB should reach El Paso in less than the estimated eight hours.

Whether or not they can do it will be influenced by the wind but of greater importance will be the quality of fuel taken on at Rockwell. The most serious problems with the motors happened when they were fueled with regular automobile gasoline. Now the tanks are filled with a new fuel made just for aeroplanes. If it's as good as the manufacturers claim, it will increase their chances for setting a non-stop record.

Weather information from the railroad people indicates this is the time of year for seasonal changes and flying at 10,000 feet is always cold. Crew members again put on their fleece-lined coats and boots. Pilots at Rockwell who regularly fly the southwestern rim of the country donate a barrel of drinking water. GMB will be flying over inhospitable country and water can determine their survival if they are forced to land.

Farewells are said, ground personnel toss coins to see which two get the honor of swinging the props, and the re-varnished fuselage fabric glistens in the morning sun as GMB turns toward the departure area.

With her fuel tanks filled to the brim, extra drums of gasoline stowed in the cargo space, and an extra drum of water, she is well over her supposed weight-carrying limit. The big motors exert their tremendous power and once again GMB lifts off slowly but smoothly. Harmon circles the field, dips the wings in salute, and turns east.

As they climb steadily toward 10,000 feet, Colonel Hartz gets out his notebook and reviews their accomplishments. There's no doubt that they have completed their Missions, and that part of his report will be easy to write. But each of the crew members has come up with recommendations for changes.

Harding and Dobias have pointed out that servicing the machine would be easier if the gasoline tanks were moved from the top of the wings to the bottom of the fuselage. They also believe the landing gear needs to be strengthened.

Lt. Harmon believes the machine would be easier to control if the vertical fins were adjusted and his suggestion that flyers should be trained to do basic maintenance, deserves consideration.

The Colonel is proud of these men. Through good times and bad they have proved to be exceptionally skilled technicians and outstanding companions. He will do whatever he can to be sure their accomplishments are noted and they get the honors they deserve.

Closing the notebook and tucking it into a pocket, he smiles and is content to let Lt. Harmon do the flying. He makes notes in the log when they fly over the Arizona towns of Yuma, Maricopa, Tucson and Douglas.

When they cross the Arizona-New Mexico border, he nudges Harmon and points to the town of Columbus. On March 9, 1916, a Mexican citizen known as Pancho Villa, burned half the town and killed 16 people.

Villa was alleged to have been a cattle thief and bandit who became a revolutionary leader when the Mexican government accepted $15,000,000 from the United States in payment for the territories of New Mexico and Utah and agreed that the Rio Grande River would be the boundary between the two nations.

In protest, Villa and his band of renegades roared across the border, raided the small settlement named Columbus, and raced back to Mexico before the United States Army could react.

Following the raid a total of eight planes were flown to Texas to help General John J. Pershing and his troops protect the border. The idea was good but the aeroplanes were not. Battered by dust storms, windstorms and snowstorms and unable to fly high enough to get over the Mexican mountains south of the border, their usefulness is restricted to courier and observation services and those assignments can only be flown in good weather.

Fortunately for GMB the weather has been perfect all the way and the following wind has provided plenty of push. Non-stop flying time from San Diego to El Paso is logged as seven hours and ten minutes.

Lt. Harmon has his record. He's a happy man as he puts GMB down on the parade ground of the Fort Bliss Military Flying field in El Paso.

Tired, stiff, chilled to the marrow of their bones, the crew shakes hands with the troops who have come out to welcome them. Routine post-flight checking is done quickly, mooring ropes are attached to stakes in the ground and the crew is escorted to the the mess hall for refreshments, and a hearty meal.

Tomorrow will be another day of routine work, another day closer to home and a day during which GMB and her crew will set another record and undergo the oddest experience of the entire flight.

STOWAWAY SEAT

Photo courtesy the Glenn L. Martin Company Museum

CHAPTER XVII

TROUBLE OVER TEXAS

November 1 through November 5

First thing in the morning Col. Hartz does two publicity flights. Border patrol aircraft take off and report back to say there's no suspicious activity on the other side of the Rio Grande. GMB is the only big excitement around Fort Bliss and when she is back on the ground, Harding and Dobias go through the routine pre-flight inspections for the benefit of the men who follow them around.

One of the followers is a 17-year-old Private named Alvin Breeland. He seems to be especially curious about where they will land next. Dobias tells him they're heading for Dallas but heavy rain is forecast so they might have to land at Fort Worth and wait out the storm.

"What's it like, flying in rain?" , Breeland asks.

Dobias answers with his usual cheerful grin. "Cold and miserable." Noting the look of shock on Breeling's face, he adds, "But our clothes shed water pretty good and if the rain is too heavy, we look for a place to land."

Private Breeland accepts the answer without comment and walks away, leaving Dobias with an impression that the question and the answer have some kind of special importance to the young man. Why that should be he can't imagine. He shrugs off the impression and continues the pre-flight routine.

One of the bungee cords on the landing gear needs to be replaced and bolts holding the fuselage support bar under the nose need to be tightened.

Col. Hartz returns from sending a wire to inform Headquarters that they are headed for Dallas, salutes the officers and men who have gathered to see them off, and steps up into the control pit to take his seat beside Lt. Harmon.

Again there is a coin toss to see who gets the honor of swinging the big wooden props, so Dobias and Harding climb into their seats and wave to the crowd. Col. Hartz signals, the props are pulled through, the motors roar back to life.

GMB moves away, gradually picking up speed, leaves the ground circles the Fort once, and turns northeast. They're off early and should easily get to Dallas ahead of the afternoon thunderstorms.

Twenty minutes out of Fort Bliss two DH4s catch up with them. Signals from the pilots indicate that GMB should return to the Fort Harmon and Hartz are puzzled. The aeroplane is performing well. Control pit instruments show no indication of problems developing But the DH pilots are insistent. Hartz shrugs, and Harmon does a 180-degree turn.

The minute GMB touches down, she is surrounded by military police and before the Colonel can get out of the control pit, two of them dart under the nose of GMB and back out, escorting a young man between them. GMB has another first to add to her long list of accomplishments. She has carried the first ever aeroplane stowaway.

Private Breeland has learned during his short month in the Army that he hates the life and wants nothing so much as to get back home to Fort Worth. Sitting on the bracing rod underneath the nose, hanging onto the struts, seemed like a good way to go.

The MPs take him away and GMB is off again, climbing to 10,300 feet, hoping to pick up a pushing wind.

Col. Hartz is on the controls and Harmon makes notes about the Texas landscape. He lists decent landing areas at Odessa, Midland, Big Spring and Sweetwater. From Cisco to Fort Worth the country is open below but the skies above are getting darker. The forecast thunderstorms are moving in fast and there is no way GMB can get to Dallas before the storms hit. Col. Hartz declares a weather emergency and lands outside Fort Worth.

He wires Headquarters: "Delayed in flight owing to bad weather and stowaway on landing gear which caused us to return to El Paso and set him off. Will proceed to Dallas tomorrow if rain stops. Then Houston and Baton Rouge."

By late afternoon the weather has moved out but the 42 mile run to Dallas takes 50 minutes.

The over night stay in Dallas is quiet and the next morning's flight to Houston is an uneventful ride over open country with plenty of good landing fields along the way.

Col. Hartz agrees to fly two demonstration flights for local newspaper people and during the last one there is trouble with the left motor and propeller.   Harding and Dobias labor until after midnight to do repairs. At dawn they are off again, heading for the Gerstner Field Flying School at Lake Charles, Louisiana.

It's a miserable two hour ride from Houston. The air is rough, intermittent rain showers are heavy, the port motor is not running the way it should, and lowering clouds indicate more bad weather ahead. The City of Lake Charles and Gerstner Field are welcome sights.

As usual GMB is surrounded by friendly and curious troops the minute she stops. Col. Hartz, and Lt. Harmon, who had been stationed at Gerstner earlier in their careers, are happily surprised to find friends still there. They will sit out the miserable weather in good company. At this point, being delayed one more day doesn't matter.

Col. Hartz wires Washington: " At Gerstner Field, Louisiana. Future destination unknown due to heavy rains."

The evening get-together is "hangar flying" at its finest. Hartz and Harmon want to hear about activities and events at Gerstner and the men stationed at the Field want to hear about the flight.

Old friends and new friends listen quietly, awed by the experiences these men have had during their flight around the perimeter of the country.   Hartz tells of the interest and cooperation from local officials who accept the importance of building air fields and marking them so there is consistency from field to field.

"Great idea," one of the Gerstner flyers says.   "But how do we find these fancy fields? Automobile maps don't indicate landing areas. What we need are maps just for pilots."

There is general agreement and one of the older pilots points out that "every pilot I know keeps his own maps of every area he's flown over. Too bad all that information can't be pulled together and made into one map that everybody could use."

Lt. Harmon responds. "Why can't it?" and Col. Hartz says "Yes. why not? We could use the automobile maps as a base and devise a set of symbols to use to indicate landing fields and what services are available."

A voice from the back of the room says, "Add notes about the surrounding territory, too. Elevations we can get from our instruments and on clear days when we have good views of the and around an airport, we can make notes about dangerous areas to watch out for."

"Yeah," someone else chimes in. "This place is a good example. A pilot who has never flown over this part of the country might not see the gas mounds. The highest one is only three feet tall. In an emergency landing they could be the difference between a crack up you walk away from and one you don't."

Someone else speaks up. "Don't forget the rice fields. They can look like good places to land when the sun is not reflecting off the water and there are drainage and irrigation ditches too. If it's raining or there's ground fog, you can't pick them out. It would be good to have them marked on a map as a danger area."

"The more I hear the better I like the idea," Col. Hartz says. "I'll include your recommendations in my final report and suggest a designated location where all this information can be sent and coordinated."

"That takes care of maps," a voice remarks. "Now if we can convince the brass that we need radios .. " There is laughter and Harmon relates his experience when he tried to get radios installed in GMB. "I'm willing to bet," he says, "that one day soon radios will be standard equipment for aeroplanes just like they are now for ships."

Col. Hartz agrees. "We will see many new services developed over the next ten years. No matter what some of the skeptics say, travel by air will one day be commonplace. What we and all the other transcontinental flyers and the pilots who fly the mails are doing is setting up the stations where aeroplanes will land people and all kinds of merchandise, in the future."

"Sounds good to me," says a voice from the rear. "But I have to fly around Gerstner Field tomorrow and I'm for bed."

Next morning Harding and Dobias find minor repairs that need doing, and they take time to explain their work to the mechanics who lend a hand . There is the routine work of checking propeller fastenings and when Dobias mentions that they're running low on cotter pins again, one of the volunteer helpers trots off and returns shortly with a full box. "A token of appreciation for telling us about the machine," he says.

The tedious but necessary work goes on. Control cables, fuselage fabric, nuts and bolts, propeller bolts, landing gear, tires, and all the hoses for water and gasoline, are carefully gone over. GMB is serviced with gasoline, water and oil, and extra supplies are loaded into the cargo compartment. They can leave any time.

Rain and wind continue and the forecast for tomorrow is not too encouraging. At the evening meeting Harmon says, "I don't mind if we have to spend another day here." The others agree that . Gerstner Field has been a pleasant stop. And they nod again when Harmon adds, "But it will be nice to get home."

Hartz outlines their route. "Next stop will be New Orleans. From there we follow the Gulf Coast to Florida , fly around the peninsula, then along the Atlantic Coast and back to Bolling Field. We should be home in four days."

"We could make it in three days if we push," Harmon says and Harding and Dobias object.

"No, let's not push. Too many little things are going wrong. Let's stick with a steady pace and make sure we get back ."

Next morning the Commanding Officer at Gerstner shakes his head. Pilots who have flown east toward Mobile and south toward Pensacola, Florida, say weather conditions to the south are very unsettled. They may get through to New Orleans but this time of year nasty storms with high winds and heavy rains form quickly in the Gulf of Mexico and spread over a wide area.

Col. Hartz points out that the Florida peninsula is part of the rim of the country so if it's possible, they must make the trip south. They've had to cope with some nasty weather along several segments of their flight. They will stick with their plan to follow the Gulf Coast to Mobile, Alabama, go east along the edge of the Florida panhandle and see what the weather looks like. .

CHAPTER XVIII

FLORIDA BY PASS

November 6 and 7

As GMB heads east, cloud build-ups force her to climb higher and higher. Upper level winds are strong and it takes three hours and 20 minutes to cover the 200 miles between Lake Charles and New Orleans. From personal knowledge and occasional breaks in the clouds, Harmon puts warnings into the flight log: "It is practically impossible to land with safety. The entire country is devoted to sugar cane and rice. Fields are very small and chopped up by ditches. A great deal of this land is flood and tide land."

Cloud cover breaks and allows them to sight the landing field half way between Lake Pontchartrain and the Mississippi River at the northwest end of the business section of New Orleans. Harmon notes that   "present condition is very poor but it is being put into fairly good shape."

Pilots at the air port tell them weather conditions to the east are not getting any better and the Stationmaster for the New Orleans and North Eastern Railroad agrees. His best guess is that practically the entire Florida peninsula is covered by storms of varying intensity. How long they will last is impossible to say.

Staying over night in New Orleans is the obvious thing to do.

Conversation around the breakfast table centers on what lies ahead. All agree they have had their fill of bad weather. They are tired, too many little things are going wrong with the aeroplane and the motors are now 50 hours beyond what the factory recommends as operating time between overhauls.

The idea of heading straight back to Bolling is sounding better all the time, but they agree they must make the attempt to complete their Mission of flying around the rim of the country. They will go east at least as far as Tallahassee.

Between New Orleans and Mobile, Alabama there are no safe landing areas. This is swamp and tide land and even those areas where there might be room enough for an emergency landing, have random growths of trees that would be impossible to miss.

Standard Oil Company maintains a landing field at Baton Rouge but it's only 2,000 square feet and that's not big enough for GMB. However, there is an excellent field two and a half miles southeast of Mobile.

Despite heavy clouds and intermittent showers, they continue east along the Gulf Coast and on across the Florida Panhandle. There is a good landing field east of Tallahassee, on top of one of the tallest hills in Florida. The field is marked with a 'T' with an American flag on top of it. It's big enough for GMB and there are services on the field, but the winds are too strong to risk a landing .

Lt. Harmon says "Let's take a chance on getting down at Jacksonville."

It's a gamble that doesn't pay off. Winds are increasing steadily. Cloud are turning black. Jacksonville is out of the question. Only on the north side of the storm is there any kind of safety.

Harmon turns GMB onto a northwest heading and as dusk darkens into nightfall, he lands them safely on the small, but well marked Maxwell Air Service Repair Station field near   Montgomery, Alabama.

In the evening the men meet to discuss their next move. Harding and Dobias point out that they cannot do much more patching on the fuselage, the tires are badly worn, and one of the wood spars has cracked and needs to be replaced. GMB is in no shape to handle turbulent weather or heavy rains. They also point out that the Repair Station has no replacement parts for GMB and ordering anything from Headquarters will mean more delays.

Colonel Hartz pulls out his much battered copy of their assigned Missions. There's no doubt that the motors and the strength of the aeroplane structure have been thoroughly tested. As for showing off their big aeroplane and encouraging local construction of landing fields, it's not that important in Florida.   Aeroplanes and flying activities of all kinds have been making history in Florida for at least 15 years.

All things considered, a flight around the outer edges of the state won't produce any information that's worth risking their necks for. Col. Hartz makes his decision:

" Let's go home."

CHAPTER XIX

MISSIONS ACCOMPLISHED

November 8 and 9

First thing Saturday morning the railroad people tell Col. Hartz the nasty weather in Florida is moving north. He wires Headquarters:

"Have cancelled Florida circuit.   Landing at Tallahassee and at Jacksonville out of question due to high winds.   Will proceed north from Montgomery. Expect to arrive at Bolling on November 9."

It's nearly a thousand miles from Montgomery to Bolling Field and Hartz and Harmon have flown over this part of the country often enough to know there are plenty of good landing areas along the way.   Just to keep the records straight, they continue making notes in the log: "Around Columbus and Fort Valley, Georgia there are plenty of fair fields within easy gliding distance.   Macon has an excellent field at   race track southwest of City. At Augusta there is an excellent field on the parade ground which is   surrounded by open country."

The flight moves on across South Carolina. The cities of Columbia and Charleston have ample landing fields but there is no reason to make use of them. The   motors are running smoothly and the weather is good.   They should reach Bolling Field, as Col. Hartz promised, on November 9th.   That's tomorrow and the crisp cold air at 5,600 feet is bearable for one more day.

As they angle northeast   Lt. Harmon   points to a distant line of clouds.   Col.Hartz checks the map.   The City below is Pinehurst, North Carolina. There is an excellent field due south of the town. and GMB has been in the air five and a half hours.

"Let's land and get gasoline," he says.

While the aeroplane is being serviced, Lt. Harmon talks with one of the local pilots and reports to Col. Hartz.:

"Raleigh's only about 72 miles. We could make it before dark." He glances at the increasing clouds still hanging out to the east. "If we beat the storm we'll be that much closer to home. "

Col. Hartz nods. Harding and Dobias finish filling fuel tanks and checking oil and water. They swing the props and hurry back to their seats. GMB takes off for Raleigh at top speed. But the storm is moving faster than they are. Half way to Raleigh the increasingly rough air and flashes of lightning force GMB to turn back to Pinehurst for the night.

<u>November 9</u>

Through the night the storm blows itself out and morning presents a perfect day for flying. Home and Bolling Field are only 500 miles to the northeast.

The motors maintain their steady roar and the air is smooth as Raleigh slides by below. Ahead are Emporia and Richmond, Virginia. The countryside is thickly wooded and there are cultivated fields where emergency landings could be made.

But there is no need for an emergency landing. Beyond Richmond the Potomac River leads to Washington, D.C. GMB touches down gently on Bolling Field

It's Sunday and the crew doesn't expect a brass band but it is a disappointment that there's is no brass of any kind to welcome them back. Only the base photographer is there.

Col. Hartz asks one of the men about Gen. Mitchell and learns that Mitchell had left on a special assignment the preceding Friday.

GMB is moored in the same spot she had left three and a half months earlier and the photographer asks them to line up for a picture.

Harding and Dobias go through the usual post-flight routines, Col. Hartz and Lt. Harmon help unload the cargo compartment, and sort personal gear . They shake hands, salute, and go their separate ways.

The lack of special welcome is not important. Each man carries his own pride and knowledge of a job well done. An assignment intended to test a machine and set up the beginning of the future of air travel, has ended with all missions accomplished.

HOME AGAIN

Left to right: Sergeant "Jack" Harding; Sergeant "Jerry" Dobias; 1st Lt. "Tiny" Harmon; and Lt. Col. R. S. Hartz.

Photo courtesy the Merle C. Olmsted Collection.

EPILOGUE

During the following week Col. Hartz files a detailed report of the flight. He includes recommendations for changes in GMB and the development of idea for tools and services.

His recommendations for changes in the aeroplane itself are carefully evaluated by the Air Service engineering people at McCook Field and the staff at the Glenn Martin factory in Cleveland. As a result GMB is designated MB-1 and the second version of the Glenn Martin Bomber, labeled MB-2, becomes the standard bomber used by the Air Service during the 1920's.

Other Hartz recommendations urge the creation and development of standard equipment for flyers. Special maps are already being worked on, but his report speeds up development of aeronautical charts, aviation weather service, clearly defined air routes, the basics of flight planning, consistent designs and markings for air ports and landing areas, ground service facilities, distribution systems for aviation gasoline and oil, radio communication gear, heated cockpits, pilot relief tubes, and training in aeroplane maintenance for pilots.

Recognition of the value of cooperation between the railroads and aeroplane crews for routing and weather information is strongly recommended and this cooperation will become the foundation for development of airline companies and scheduled air service.

Shortly after his formal report and recommendations are turned in, Col. Hartz receives the following memorandum:

"Director of Air Service commends you as Commanding Officer, and members of your crew, namely 2nd Lt. Ernest E. Harmon,

EPILOGUE – Continued

Assistant Pilot, Master Signal Electricians Jack Harding and Jerry Dobias, both mechanics, for having successfully completed the mission on which you started out. Signed: I. Westover, Colonel "

Some six weeks after her return to Bolling Field, GMB/MB-1 is flown back to McCook Field in Dayton, Ohio. There she is converted into a transport with 12 seats inside the fuselage. For the next couple years she carries the McCook baseball team and other VIPs around the country.

She is only four years old when aeronautical progress ends her usefulness.

GMB/MB-1 disappears. Rumor says she has been disassembled, crated and shipped to a museum where historically significant aircraft are being collected and warehoused. The museum says she never arrived.

Despite her short life and the uncertainty of her fate, GMB and the crew that took her on the flight around the rim of the United States, in 1919, deserve center stage, with spotlights, in the drama of aviation history.

The challenges they met, the obstacles they overcame, and the courage that made their accomplishments possible, are the stuff of legends and a legacy forever.

GLOSSARY

The language of aviation has remained reasonably static despite the growth and sophistication the industry has undergone. In an attempt to maintain the early days mood of this story, the author has used words and spellings which were then in common usage.

Listed here are those words and their modern counterparts.

Aeroplane	Airplane

Aeroplane Landing Field – a public-use facility where aeroplanes are permitted to land, i.e., public park, golf course, race track, etc.

Air Port	Airport
Army Air Service	United States Air Force
Control Pit	Cockpit
Departure Area	Runway
Departure Run	Take-off
Flight Record Book	Log Book
Gasoline	Avgas
Inclinometer	Attitude Indicator
Landing Field	Any open area
Motor	Engine
Runway	Taxiway

GLOSSARY - Continued

Three Point Landing .. a maneuver during which the front wheels and the tail skid touch the ground at the exact same moment.

Wind on the Nose   Headwind

Wind at your back   Tailwind

MILITARY ABBREVIATIONS

ASA – Air Service, Army

JMA – Junior Military Aviator .. first rating received

MA – Military Aviator .. rating eared after three years of flying

RMA – Reserve Military Aviator .. rating for regular Army Officer

CIVILIAN ABBREVIATIONS

AAHS –American Aviation Historical Society

AOPA – Aircraft Owners and Pilots Association

AWA – Aviation Writers' Association

FAA – Federal Aviation Administration

FAMA –Florida Airport Managers' Association

FATA – Florida Aviation Trades Association

NATA – National Air Transportation Association

NBAA – National Business Aviation Association

SELECTED BIBLIOGRAPHY

As anyone who has done any kind of research is well aware, bits of useful information are often found in sources not directly related to the subject under investigation. For that reason this bibliography cannot be a total and complete listing of every piece of printed material the author chanced to read.

However, all major sources are included and will provide sources for further reading by those among you who are interested in the days, the times, and the people, who created the air transportation industry we have today.

Books

Aircraft Yearbook. New York: :Aeronautical Chamber of Commerce of America, Inc., 1920, 1921, 1922

Andrist, Ralph K. and Editors of American Heritage. *History of the Confident Years.* New York: American Heritage Publishing Co., Inc.

Bower, Ezra and the Editors of Time-Life Books. *Knights of the Air.* Alexandria, VA: Time-Life Books 1980

Bruns, James H. *Tuck Bird –The High Flying Life and Times of Eddie Gardner.* Washington,D.C.: National Postal Museum, Smithsonian Institution 1998

Chatfield, C.H., S.M., C. Fayette Taylor, M.E., and Shatswell Ober, S.B.. *The Airplane and Its Engine-Third Edition.* New York: McGraw-Hill Book Co., Inc. 1936

Cunningham, William Glenn. *The Aircraft Industry.* Los Angeles: Lorrin L. Morrison 1951

Daniel, Clifton, Editor in Chief. *The 20th Century Day By Day, 1999 Edition.* New York. DK Publishing, Inc. First published 1987 as *Chronicles of the 20th Century*

Davis, Burke. *The Billy Mitchell Affair.* New York: Random House 1967

Dickey, Phillip S., III, Lt. Col., USAF (Ret.). *The Liberty Engine, 1918-1942. Vol. 1 No. 3.* Washington, D.C.: Smithsonian Institution Press, 1968

Donald, David. General Editor. *The Complete Book of World Aircraft.* New York. Barnes & Noble 1997

Dyke, Al. *Dyke's Aircraft Engine Instruction.* Chicago: Goodheart & Wilcox Co., Inc. 1928

Dwiggins, Don. *The Barnstormers.* New York: Grossett & Dunlop. 1968

Emme, Eugene M., NASA Historian. *Aeronautics & Astronautics.* Washington: Government Printing Office. 1961

Feeny, William D.. *In Their Honor.* New York: Duell, Sloan and Pearce. 1963

Gardner, Lester D. *Who's Who in American Aeronautics, Second Edition 1925.* Los Angeles: Reproduction by Floyd Clymer

Gauvreance, Emile and Lester Cohn. *Billy Mitchell.* New York: E.P. Dutton & Co., Inc.. 1942

Goldberg, Alfred, Editor. *A History of the United States air Force.* Princeton: D. Van Nostrand Co., Inc. 1957

Grennell-Milne, Duncan. *Wind In The Wires.* London: Mayflower Books. 1966

Hart, Hubert M. *Pioneer Forts of the West.* Seattle: Superior Publishing Co. 1981

Hartz, Rutherford S., formerly Lieut. Colonel, Air Corps, U.S. Army, and Commander of the "Round the Rim of the U.S." Flight and Elzor E. Hall, Lieut, Air Corps Res., Formerly Aviation Sec. S.C., U.S. Army. *Airplane Mechanics Rigging Handbook.* New York: The Ronald Press Co. 1930

Hatfield, D. D.   *Aeroplane Scrapbook No. 3 – Amazing Developments in American Aeronautics, 1911-1941.* Inglewod: Northrup University Press. 1975.

Holland, Rupert Sargent. *Historic Airships.* Philadelphia: Macree-Smith Co. 1928

Holmes, Donald B.   *Air Mail – An Illustrated History.* New York: Clarkson N. Porter, Inc. 1981

Holbrook, Stewart H. *The Story of American Railroads.* New York: Crown Publishers. 1947

Hurley, Alfred H., Major USAF.   *Billy Mitchell, Crusader for Air Power.* New York: Franklin Watts, Inc. 1964

Ingalls, Douglas J. *The Plane That changed The World.* Fallbrook: Aero Publishers, Inc. 1961

Jane's All The World Aircraft, 1919

Josephy, Alvin M., Jr., Editor in Charge. *The American Heritage History of Flight. New York: American Heritage Publishing Co., Inc. 1962*

Klingman, William K.   *1919 – The Year Our World Began.* New York: St. Martin Press. 1987

Levine, Isaac Don. *Mitchell, Pioneer of Air Power.* New York. Duell, Sloan & Pearce. 1943

Lincke, Jack R. *Jenny Was No Lady – The Story of the JN-4D.* New York. W.W. Norton & Co., Inc. 1970

Lincoln Library of Essential Information, 1940 Edition. Buffalo: The Frontier Press Co. 1940

Loening, Grover. *Takeoff Into Greatness.* New York. G.P. Putnam's Sons, Inc. 1968 .

Mason, Herbert Molloy, Jr. *United States Air Force – A Turbulent History.* New York: Mason/Charter. 1976

Miller, John Anderson. *Fares Please. – Fourth Edition.* New York: Dover Publications, Inc.

Mitchell, William. *Winged Defense.* New York: G.P. Putnam's Sons, 1925. Dover Edition published 1988

Obregon, Maurice. *Argonauts to Astronauts.* New York: Harper & Row. 1977

Page, Victor W., Major, Air Corps Reserve USA. *Modern Aircraft.* New York: Norman W. Henry Publishing Co. 1927

Prendergast, Curtis and The Editors of Time-Life Books. *The First Aviators.* Alexandria: Time-Life Books. 1981

Reingold, Ruth. *Sky Pioneers – Arizona in Aviation History.* Tucson: The University of Arizona Press. 1982

Scamerhorn, Howard L. *Balloons To Jets.* Chicago: Henry Ragnery Co. 1957

Sill, Henry. *To Ride The Wind – A Biography of Glenn L. Martin.* New York: Julian Messner, Inc. 1964.

Sudsbury, Elretta, Editor. *Jackrabbits to Jets – 2nd Edition.* San Diego: North Island Historical Commission. 1967

Sullivan, Mack. *Our Times, 1900-1919. Vol. II – America Finding Herslf. Vol. III – Pre-War America.* New York: Charles Scribner's Sons. 1971

The Army Air Force Aid Society. *Official Guide to Army Air Forces, 1942. New York: Pocket Books, 1944*

Thomas, Lowell. *The First World Flight.* New York: Houghton Mifflin Co. 1925

Vale, John W. Jr. *Aviation Mechanics Engine Manual.* New York:McGraw-Hill Cook Co. 1946

Vecsey, Geroge and George C. Drake. *Getting Off The Ground.* New York: E.P. Dutton 1979

Wagner, Ray. *American Combat Planes, New Revised Edition.* New York: Doubleday Co., Inc. 1968

Whitehouse, Arch. *The Early Birds.* New York: Modern Library Editions Publishing Co. 1965

Wilson, Mitchell. *American Science and Invention.* New York: Bonanza Books, Division of Crown Publishers, Inc., by arrangement with Simon & Schuster, Inc. 1954

Government Printing Office

Washington, D.C. 1919. *Air Service Information Circular No. 2*

Washington, D.C. 1968. *Annals of Flight, Vol. 1, No. 3 – The Liberty Engine 1918-1942.* Smithsonian Institution

Washington, D.C. 1960. Department of Commerce. *Historical Statistics of the United States, Colonial Times to 1957.*

Washington, D.C. 1956. Heflin, Woodford Agee, Editor. *The United States Air Force Dictionary.* Air University Press

Washington, D.C. 1956. Hunsaker, J.C. From the Smithsonian Report for 1955, Pages 241-271. *Forty Years of Aeronautical Research.*

Washington, D.C. 1978 and 1979. Mauer, Mauer Editor. *The U.S* *Air Service in World War I. Volume I – The Final Report and a* *Tactical History. Volume II – Early Concept of Military Aviation* *Volume III – The Battle of San Mihiel.* The Alfred F. Simpson Historical Research Center, Maxwell AFB, Alabama, The Office o Air Force History, Headquarters USAF

Government Offices

Various Documents from the files of The National Archives, The Library of the National Air and Space Museum, the Alfred F Simpson Historical Research Center, Maxwell AFB, Alabama, and The Office of Air Force History, Headquarters, USAF.

Periodicals

Aerial Age Weekly, May 31, 1920

Aerospace Historian, Volume 20, June 1973, September 1973: Volume 23, June 1976

American Heritage, Volume XV, No. 6, Volume XXI, No. 1

American Heritage Illustrated, December 1974

Aviation Engineering, December 1931

Aviation Magazine, January 1919

Journal of the American Aviation Historical Society, Volumes 1, 2, 4, 5, 6, 7, 8, 11, 14, 15, 46

National Glider and Airplane News, May 1931

Popular Mechanics, November 1, 1919

Scientific American, Vol. 118, No. 22, Vol. 119, No. 23

The Airpower Historian, Vol. III, No. 3, Vol. VI, No. 3

The American Review of Reviews, Vol. LX, No. 355

Miscellaneous Sources

American Aviation Historical Society (The), Santa Ana, CA

Documents and photographs from the Merle C. Olmsted Collection

Engineering Library, University of Arizona, Tucson, AZ

Frederick Cradford Auto-Aviation Museum, Cleveland, OH

Glenn L. Martin Aviation Museum (The), Baltimore, MD

Martin-Marietta Company (The), Baltimore, MD

Memories and memorabilia from the family of Jerry Dobias

Million Magazines, Tucson, AZ

Pima Air and Space Museum, Tucson, AZ

Public Library, Mesa, AZ

Research Department, Public Library, Tucson, AZ

San Diego Aeronautical Museum (The), San Diego, CA

United States Air Force Museum (The), Dayton, OH

My fascination with flying began with the first training session in one of Bill Piper's J-3 Cubs and continued through cockpit time in one of Bill Lear's Model 23 business jets.

Jobs in the aviation industry began at the switchboard in the Flight Office, Sky Harbor Airport, Northbrook, Illinois, moved south to an assignment as Public Relations Officer, Fort Lauderdale Executive Airport (FXE) and continued through five years as Executive Director, Florida Aviation Trades Association.

Volunteer efforts included work with the Broward County Transportation Committee, the Aviation Committee of the Fort Lauderdale Chamber of Commerce, and 13 years as a member of the State of Florida Aviation Advisory Council.

Being an "aviation writer" generated uncountable opportunities to meet the men and women whose daily activities involved every kind of aerial machine and touched every part of the aviation industry. Their tales, tall and small, inspired a curiosity about the men and women of earlier times .. the pioneers who established the foundations of our modern air transportation industry. Research into aviation history became, and remains, a passion.

It is my sincere hope that you have enjoyed my attempt to bring to light the saga of one aeroplane, one crew, and one flight too long buried in the dust of history.

Miriam O. Seymour